YOUTUBE PLAY BOOK 2020

A PRACTICAL STEP-BY-STEP GUIDE TO ALL THINGS
YOUTUBE RELATED. THIS INCLUDES STARTING A
CHANNEL, OPTIMIZING IT, GROWING A
FOLLOWING, AND MONETIZING IT

BRANDON'S BUSINESS GUIDES

CONTENTS

INTRODUCTION

A few years ago, after dedicating a significant amount of time into blogging, I decided to try out something different. I wanted to keep my growing audience captivated and at the same time, bring in more of a personal touch to the content I was creating. Many online gurus were emphasizing the importance of creating video content, and based on the statistics that were showing up five years ago, I started to take video creation seriously. Then I came across the story of Gary Vee and how he gained a lot of fame by drinking four bottles of wine every day on his YouTube channel, which resulted in growing his family business as well as his own name. At that point, I realized it was time for me to act.

At first, I started creating video content and hosting

it on YouTube, so I could share it with my blog followers. The intention was to easily embed into the written content that I was consistently creating.

It quickly evolved into creating long-form video content, which is today commonly referred to as "vlogging." After about eighteen months of this, I decided it was time to go all-in with my YouTube channel. The initial strategy of embedding videos on my blog post did reasonably well. I was able to keep people engaged, and increased interaction on my blogs, but the YouTube channel was a ghost town. I could see other leaders with crazy numbers and engagement levels on their YouTube channels, and I didn't get why nothing was growing for me. And I mean nothing!

Three years into creating videos and hosting them on YouTube, I kid you not, my subscriber count as a whopping 27 people. That sucked for me.

So if you've been doing this for a few months or a year and it feels like you're just hitting crickets, trust me, I have been there. I know how it feels. Part of the reason I am so excited you picked up this book is because I intend to share with you valuable information that will save you time and aspirin money because I already made all the mistakes. You can learn from my mistakes and avoid certain pitfalls.

So you want to be a YouTube Superstar?

Well, you're not alone. YouTube is an integral part of today's society, and there are a lot of content producers, most of whom aren't making much money from their efforts. I used to belong to that camp about five years ago, by the way. The good news is anyone can go from making no money to making loads of cash on YouTube. This book is going to show you how I did it and how you can too.

And when I say loads of cash, I really mean it. The potential to make money you never thought was possible (think outrageous cash with private jets and global travel to exotic islands) is not only plausible, but some've already demonstrated including me.

Quite a number of people have been able to turn a simple YouTube channel into a highly paid platform. What's even better is that you're not late to the party. And it doesn't really matter what niche market you jump into. There's content on almost any topic under the sun. Those that are making millions on YouTube are all over the map, so there's no one size fits, but the one thing they all have in common is their unique, entertaining personality and commitment to success. The YouTubers who hit it big are sitting comfortably in the upper 1% of the global elite and bringing in millions.

Am I saying you're going to make 20 million dollars like Ryan, the seven-year-old kid who was the highest YouTube earner in 2018? Or that you'll become the next Jacksepticeye (made $16M in 2018) and PewDiePie, who also cashed in over 15 million dollars in 2018? Of course not! I have no way of guaranteeing that. What I know for sure is that you don't need to have 95K subscribers like ex-gamer turned influencer PewDiePie to create a nice six-figure income and reach millions of people each year.

This book is structured in a specific way to enable you to go from zero to whatever your ideal number is. If you want to be an influencer, an industry expert, a thriving business owner, or celebrity, what I am about to teach you will make that possible with the least amount of friction.

Going back to my story of three years and only twenty-seven subscribers, a critical lesson that I learned the hard way that I need you to understand from the get-go is this:

If you want YouTube to work for you, you must be willing to put in the effort and approach it as it's own business machine. The mistake I made is I was expecting it to work for me when I was using it as merely a hosting platform where I was storing my videos to embed on my blog. What got me to make that shift and commit to understanding YouTube was an opportunity that came about thanks to the content I had been creating for my blog. A micro-influencer came across my video presentation that I had done for my blog post and found it super valuable. So much so that he referenced my video in one of his videos, which led to a massive spike on my native video views on YouTube. In other words, I got a taste of how much attention there was on YouTube. In all my years of blogging and growing my followers, the impact that single video brought was 10X bigger than anything I had experienced prior. People commented and asked questions within the YouTube community, which lead to a few follow up conversations, and that caused me to go on a learning frenzy.

I started learning everything I could on how to grow a YouTube channel, how it works, and what other successful YouTube creators were doing. I went from no momentum to a lot of momentum within a few months. It took me years to get my first 30 subscribers, and within 24 months, I was getting hundreds of thousands of views a month and was up to ninety thousand subscribers. This was just the start for me, and the rest has been one incredible adventure. The tough lessons learned as well as how I started making 10K a month are some of the secrets I will be sharing throughout this book so make sure you feel ready to go all-in because I can promise to deliver if you promise to commit and execute.

YouTube is really not for everyone:

Not everyone who gets started on YouTube is going to turn it into a profitable platform for their objectives. In fact, we are told that one in ten beginners never make it past that first significant milestone of 1000 subscribers. Most people quit because that first milestone is tough. And even for those that make it to over a thousand, few ever actually manage to monetize and earn decent money from it. Even fewer make it to the 100,000-subscriber milestone where YouTube gives you a dedicated channel advisor, and you make enough money to make this fulltime.

The hard truth is that YouTube favors more prominent channels. The vast majority of channels are those with under a thousand subscribers because the odds are stacked against beginners and smaller channels. So the best you can do is to grow and get to those big numbers as fast as possible, especially if you want this to become your full-time career.

Brenda shared that she'd been stuck at 650 subscribers for about a year, and it was starting to demoralize her creative efforts because she didn't feel like anything she tried was working. Part of this is due to the fact that YouTube doesn't favor small channels, as we said. But some of it also had to do with the mistakes I will be dissecting in the next chapter.

This book is definitely for you:

Whether you are a beginner with zero subscribers and just setting up your channel now or if like Brenda, you already have a channel but feel stuck and unable to build that momentum that will lead to monetization and impact, this book is for you. We are going to briefly cover the basics of getting started and then jump right into the heart of winning the YouTube game. And that is, growing, optimizing and monetizing your YouTube channel.

After reading this book you will not only have the information necessary to grow your channel, you'll also have the right mindset that will enable you to overcome some of the obstacles that prevent many YouTubers from succeeding. That includes how to make the platform work for you even when you're not yet a big player with thousands of subscribers. As YouTube continues to grow and video content continues to be the most consumed content, there's never been a more opportune time for you to create the kind of financial freedom you've always dreamed of than today. All it takes is an investment in yourself to read this entire book, implement and develop the necessary money-making skills.

What you'll learn in this book:

- How to get lots of views even if you have zero subscribers.
- How to keep your content idea bank full of the best stuff and also hack the most popular videos in your topic for faster success.
- The biggest mistakes aspiring YouTubers make that sabotages their success.
- The growth hack every successful YouTuber is using so that you can optimize and take your channel to the next level.

And so much more...

If you have been looking for a single resource that can help you succeed and become a superstar on this mature and competitive platform, this is it. Let's not waste any more time.

SECTION ONE: THE BASICS

GETTING STARTED

Over a billion people on the Internet are using YouTube to discover, consume, and share video content. We are told that users consumer one billion hours a day. Now that is a lot of attention. Imagine how different life would be for you if you could only get a tiny percentage of that attention consistently. In this section, we are going to quickly cover some of the basics for the absolute newbies who need to know how to set up your channel, the equipment you need, and all that essential stuff that you need to be successful. In the next section, we shift gears because I want to bring more value to people who already have the basics down and perhaps even have subscribers coming in. Before we get into any of that, how about a brief history of YouTube and why you should invest in building out your channel.

A brief history and some statistics every YouTuber should know:

Three former PayPal employees founded YouTube in 2005 in an office garage. Chad Hurley, Steven Chen and Jawed Karim created the service in February of 2005. A year after its inception, it was already attracting more than 65,000 new video uploads and 100 million video views per day. This led to a life-altering opportunity for the founders because, in November 2006, the start-up was acquired for over $1 billion by Google.

Since then, YouTube has opened up avenues for brands to advertise on their videos, and in turn, content creators have been able to earn a living just by making videos. This is one of the main reasons content creators invest a lot of time and effort in producing engaging videos and hosting them natively on the platform. The result of this is that YouTube is now the second most trafficked website and the second largest search engine in the world.

According to Hubspot, there are 400hours of video content uploaded to YouTube every minute. One billion hours of videos are watched on YouTube every day. There are over 1.9 billion monthly active logged-in users. YouTube is available in more than 91 countries, in 80 different languages, and 68% of YouTube users say they watched a video to help them make a purchase decision. Four times as many people prefer watching videos on YouTube rather than on social media platforms. The number of YouTubers who earn a six-figure income per year has increased by more than 40% since 2017. Over half of American Internet users who are aged 75 and above prefer to watch videos on YouTube. Lastly, 90% of 18-44-year-old American Internet users watch videos on YouTube. These are just a few of the statistics we know about YouTube and how it's dominating the Internet.

Why should you care or go all-in with your YouTube marketing?

Contrary to what you'll hear, a lot of marketers say, YouTube is not dead. I repeat, YouTube is not dead. In fact, there's a good argument that YouTube won't be fading our like so many other income strategies do because of the nature and infrastructure of the platform. Despite the 400+ hours of video content being uploaded every minute and over twenty-three million channels on YouTube, it will always be a money-making platform for those who have the right strategy in place. That's why you should go all in.

This isn't about convincing you because by reading this book, I can already tell you've made the decision to make it work, but there will be times when things get tough. Times when you might start questioning if it's really worth the effort and commitment, especially if you happen to come across a frustrated creator who hasn't experienced any success. And when that moment comes, and you hear, "YouTube is dead," I want you to delete that information immediately. Don't buy into that kind of thinking. Read this book and trust in the process and your own journey. The strategy laid out in this book will get you the results you desire.

Mistakes new YouTubers make when starting out:

The biggest reason most people fail is that they give up too soon. They allow overwhelming, frustration, and impatience to kick in. No one has ever become successful online without going through the ropes, overcoming obstacles, and exercising a lot of patience.

Your solution: Don't give up. Never allow frustration or lack of momentum to discourage you. Remember, I had only 27 subscribers for a really long time. My mentor shares a story of how, when he started, he had zero subscribers and zero video views. He kept on refreshing the screen, hoping to generate some more views by watching his own video a couple of times.

Another big mistake new YouTubers make is that they don't respect the nature of the Platform. By this, I mean the fact that YouTube is the second largest search engine on the Internet, and it is owned by the first largest search engine on the Internet. Therefore although it is a social platform, it certainly doesn't work like Facebook, Instagram, or Twitter. People go into YouTube with a certain mindset and defined expectations. When you create content, you must bear this in mind. Repurposing content on YouTube is a bad idea if you're serious about becoming a YouTube influencer. Content that works well on Twitter or Instagram or Facebook may not do as well on YouTube because entertainment or inspiration for the sake of it cannot work for a beginner who doesn't yet have an active community. So many newbies start with inspirational content or entertaining topics that they are interested in. This makes it so hard for that content to be discovered and seen, which often leads to feeling stuck.

Your solution: As you start this journey, focus on creating searchable content. People don't go into Facebook or Instagram and type key terms on the search bar, but they do on YouTube. As such, your content must be keyword-friendly. When you create your content strategy, make sure you do keyword research using the Google Keyword Planner for some ideas on phrases that people are searching for on the Internet. Only after you've gained some momentum and enough subscribers can you start creating content that's inspirational and tailored to your taste. And please, don't make the mistake of repurposing content from your other social platforms. Create content that is specifically structured for this platform.

Trying to copy and be like successful YouTube Influencers. I know it's all too easy to copy someone you already admire who has over a million subscribers, but that is the best way to kill your chances of success. Trying to be like someone else just because you see them winning only makes you a cheap copycat and turns your ideal audience away. It's called "You" Tube for a reason!

Your solution: Play to your strengths and stop comparing yourself with others who have been there for years. You may not have the professional studio set up or jokes that make everyone laugh, but you have strengths that people will resonate with. It's your job to find and play to your strengths. The more of yourself you can be, the more authentic your message, and the more you keep things real with your audience, the easier it will be to build a connection and grow your channel.

Lack of consistency. This is a big one for all of us. I struggled with this a lot, so trust me, if it feels hard; I've been there too. I used to have a full-time job, a blog, and I was still working to build my YouTube channel. Publishing content consistently that is tailor-made for my ideal audience was such a struggle I decided to start batching up my content creation process.

Your solution: Start batching up your content creation and schedule out the content in at least two weeks in advance to make sure you always have content going out at the right time. This will help train your new subscribers, and it also looks professional when potential subscribers come to your channel and learn that you consistently publish fresh content.

Making selfish content. A lot of people who come into the YouTube game only do so for the short-term gain or the idea of being famous. There's nothing wrong with wanting to be famous and make a lot of money, but that cannot be the main reason you produce content. Another big mistake is producing content that is a modified version of a press release. Self-promotional content will cause your channel to fail really fast. Remember, people will only engage with your content and become subscribers and loyal fans because of the value you deliver. Unless you can create resonance and make the viewer feel like you genuinely care about them, your videos won't do well no matter how hard you try.

Your solution: Deliver value first. Always start by thinking about why people are on YouTube and what they are looking to experience when they come across your video. Then give them exactly that. A good rule of thumb to follow comes from the advice I got from Gary Vee. Gary says it's better to synthe-size your thought process and decide whether the video is going to be entertainment or education. If you are fortunate enough to be in a niche where you can combine both, then, by all means, do that.

Not engaging and responding to comments. Benji Travis said, "If the content is the heart of YouTube, then the community is the soul of YouTube. That means you must reply to every comment you get on your video. It's always so painful for me to come across a channel where the owner has ignored comments that people left on his or her video. When people see you're not relatable and engaging, they will stop interacting or watching your videos.

Your solution: Reply to most, if not all, your comments. It shows people that you are real, authentic, and that you actually care. Influence and loyalty on YouTube are built through direct engagement.

A few YouTube Myths we have to bust:

Myth #1: YouTube is dead, and it's too late for you to start a channel and succeed.

Truth: YouTube is not dead or overcrowded, and it's certainly not too late for you to succeed. Regardless of the current statistics and number of channels and creators, the fact of the matter is there are so many new people connecting to the Internet and discovering the power of YouTube for the first time. So yeah, more creators are coming into the game, but there are also more viewers joining the platform. Competition is not a bad thing, and in a world with eight billion humans, inevitably, there will be enough of an audience for you to grow your brand and succeed as more people discover the platform.

Myth #2: You can't make money with a small YouTube channel.

Truth: Technically speaking, I have already proven this to be a myth. I don't have millions of subscribers, and I consistently make thousands of dollars each month. I have many friends who are also YouTube marketers with less than 10,000 subscribers making a comfortable living.

I even want to challenge that old thinking that you must have over a thousand subscribers and four thousand hours before you will ever make a dime. To become a YouTube influencer, you do need a tribe, but to make money on YouTube, there's more than AdSense. AdSense is simply the standard way of making money on the platform. There are other options of cashing in big, which I will be teaching you about step by step in the section on monetization. So if money is a motivator, bust that myth and get ready to make real money, really fast on YouTube by working smart and putting in the right effort.

Myth #3: Success on YouTube is predicated on natural talent.

Truth: The fact of the matter is everyone who is a thriving YouTube influencer today has crappy first videos. No one is born naturally talented on camera. The first pieces of content do suck compared to the video content you produce six months down the line. This idea of natural talent on camera is a myth that you need to bust. It takes time and practice to get to a place where your video looks fantastic, so don't stress about being perfect right off the bat. It does help if you can watch yourself back and learn a few tricks, such as focusing on the lens of the camera and remembering to smile and blink. But aside from those simple tricks, most of it comes from practice and enough preparation before going on camera so that what comes out of your mouth is such great value people don't mind how awkward you look. On YouTube, it's not about being an actor or actress. It's not about talent. It is about value.

Regardless of natural talent, skills, I.Q, race, ethnicity, nationality, or any other factor you might be thinking is a shortcoming, people have created a channel and succeeded across various niches. That means you can, too, if you put in the work, have the right strategy, and persist. These are just a few myths that I wanted to bust about succeeding on YouTube. Now let's get your channel set-up the right way.

2

QUICKSTART FOR SETTING UP YOUR CHANNEL

You can easily find in-depth guides and video tutorials on how to set up a YouTube channel so I will not spend too much time on such details. But I will guide you through some of the procedural stuff as well as some insider secrets that'll make your channel more successful right off the bat. Even if you've already set up your channel, it's well worth it going through this chapter, as you never know what small insight you might pick up that could make all the difference to your existing account.

You will also find extra recommended video resources at the end of this book to help you go through the first beginner steps if you don't have a channel set up already. Now, let's make sure the YouTube gods start smiling down on you and send views your way by setting up your channel the right way.

There are four things you need before setting up your channel:

1. The right mindset
2. The right channel name
3. The right strategy
4. A YouTube Journal (or a notes app on your phone, but I really encourage you to get a note-taking pad and pen.)

The right mindset.

In other words, your channel needs to have a clearly defined purpose, and you need to know yourself enough to figure out what you can deliver. Don't try to be a jack-of-all-trades; it will only slow down your growth and opportunities. To make YouTube work, you need to name and hone your talent and appeal to your particular market. It can be too easy to spread yourself thin, trying to produce content on varying topics that you feel might attract your audience. Chances are, going in this direction will only dilute your channel and hurt your ability to reach that first 1000 subscribers.

Another important aspect of this is approaching this with the long-view. If you want instant gratification, you will lose on YouTube. Nothing good is ever built in a day, so get rich quick cannot be your mindset. If you have invested time and energy getting your head right, then it's time to prep yourself with the other two.

Choosing the right name for your YouTube channel.

The name you choose for your channel is critical because it's what people will associate you with. The name you choose must be relevant, readable, and, if possible catchy or at least easy to recall. The shorter the title, the better. If you are building a brand around your YouTube, make sure the name you choose aligns with the rest of the brand identity. Create a sense of congruency if you have a website and other social media channels. I like to encourage my clients to either use their name or choose a name that expresses the core message of the channel.

An excellent way to get your creative juices flowing when name searching is to write down words that best describe you and what you want to achieve with this channel. Think about words that describe the type of content you'll be publishing. Mix things up by adding words that are personality-based, especially if your ideal audience is going to be niched down by demographics. Now play around with the words on your list until something cool pops.

In case you need some inspiration for your name, check out the tool called Spinxo to help you find the perfect name that defines you and your channel.

The right strategy.

You need to be strategic about your YouTube channel; otherwise, you're flying blind, and it will be really tough knowing what's working and what's wasting time.

Part of the reason I was stuck with my channel is that I wasn't executing on a growth strategy, so nothing was ever going to change. By reading this book, you'll already be ahead of the game because most newbies never take the time to educate themselves and form a gameplan. But we all know every athlete gets into the game fully prepared; otherwise, they won't stand a chance against the competition. Think of this moment now as your prep time before you step into the game. The more you leverage the strategies and tactics shared in this book, the higher your chances of creating success at half the time it took those of us who didn't know any better.

A good friend of mine who is also a beauty influencer on YouTube said it so well. She said it took her seven years to get to 50,000 subscribers. Then in less than a year, she went from 50K to 300K not because unicorns sprinkled a magic sauce on her channel, but because for that one year, she executed a carefully mapped out and intentional strategy.

I want to make sure you start out with the strategy, so you don't waste as much time as the rest of us have over the years trying to "wing it."

A YouTube Journal.

Scientific research shows that writing things down is very instrumental in executing something. Journaling down this process and actively taking notes as ideas come to you will enable you to work through what you need to do in order to become a YouTube superstar. Writing down your goals, the problems you want to solve, the business you want to have actually signals to your brain that "this is important." Your reticular activating system (RAS) then flags relevant opportunities and tools to help you achieve set goals. By choosing to be proactive as we go through this book together and the action steps provided, you essentially map out a self-customized blueprint and increase the likelihood of achieving YouTube success.

It will also spark your creativity, especially as we go through brainstorming sessions in the chapters that are to come. If you would like to learn more about the psychology behind this act of journaling down your thoughts and goals, I recommend checking out Thai Nguyen, and his blog "The Utopian Life." Now that you've have primed your-self for success with these four things, it's time to roll up your sleeves and develop your YouTube channel.

Creating your YouTube Channel:

Step One: Create a Google account.

Head over to Google or, better yet, YouTube and click "sign-in." If you have an existing Gmail account, you will be prompted to sign in with that one, alternatively just follow the onscreen instruc-tions to sign up for a new Gmail account. In the top right corner of the screen, once you've signed up, you will be able to spot a "settings" cog icon. Click to create your channel.

Step Two: Create and fill out the details of your YouTube Channel.

That includes choosing your channel icon, channel art, channel description, etc. You will also choose whether you want to create a channel using a business name, a personal name, or another. Depending on whether you are starting this as a product, brand, company, or other, the instructions are simple and easy to follow.

Now that you've signed in and created the channel, you can click on the user icon in the top right corner for the channel menu. Here you can navigate to your channel, switch accounts, and go to your channel dashboard for further customization.

Step Three: Add extra details such as links, contact details, and a trailer. To help your audience quickly access the other marketing avenues of your business, I suggest you add links to your YouTube channel. So if you have a website or another social media platform that you want to drive traffic to and vice versa, this is a great tip. YouTube allows you to choose how many links will appear on your channel art. I also recommend adding your contact details in the "About" section of your channel. It makes it easier for people to follow up with you or even inquire about your products or services once they get a good taste of the value you bring. When it comes to adding a channel trailer, although most newbies tend to overlook this part, I have found it to be hugely influential when attracting new viewers. Channel trailers auto-play whenever new people who aren't yet subscribers land on your channel. It can be an excellent opportunity to grab a viewer's attention, give them a clear picture of who you are and the value they can expect to get. That means you need to be thoughtful about the piece of content that goes here. Make it short, to-the-point, and memorable.

Insider tip:

Within your dashboard, you will find the community link where you can respond, delete or flag comments as spam. You can access the comments from your panel by going into your creator studio. I encourage you to actively respond to every comment so that people can feel like interacting with you whenever you post a new video.

You also have the ability to adjust the community settings. Add moderators to help review comments if necessary, hold comments that include links or hashtags so you can review them before they go public. Regularly check potentially inappropriate chat messages, especially during Live stream.

Step Four: Upload your first video. Before you upload that first piece of content that will launch you into the world, read the privacy policy to avoid getting your channel shut down. When it comes to publishing videos, you have a few privacy settings options. The video can be public (everyone can access it), unlisted (only people with the link can access it), private (only you can view it), scheduled (release it on a specific date in the future). When starting out, I recommend selecting "Private" to ensure you don't mess up or upload the wrong video. Once you feel ready, you may switch the video settings to public.

One last thing to remember here is that each video needs to be optimized for success. That includes thumbnails, titles, descriptions, and tags. Let's touch on each a bit more.

Thumbnails - Given the fact that this is what new viewers will see first, it is an excellent idea to custom make your own thumbnails. Don't get too fussy about it, but put some effort into it. Customizing your thumbnails helps give your channel brand coherency and a professional look. It can also be a great way to stand out on a YouTube search if people type in your keywords.

Tags - Speaking of keywords, in YouTube land, keywords, and phrases or questions that people are typing in the search box must become core to your video optimization. People go to YouTube in search of something. The more you can include in the tags section keywords that your ideal audience is typing, the easier it will be for your video to show up on their feed. Long-tail keywords are the way to go, in my opinion, but make sure whatever words you use, the video itself can actually deliver on those search terms. Don't just lure in people for the sake of getting views; otherwise, people will complain, and Google may penalize you. To add multiple keywords, type in your phrase in the "Tags" field, then add a comma or hit enter to confirm.

Title - You have about seventy characters to state your compelling message. Be concise and as descriptive as you can about the content of the video you are posting so that people know what to expect. Your video title should give a potential viewer an enticing reason to click through. This doesn't mean clickbait titles or misleading information. It should be congruent with the thumbnail image you created.

For example, Do Not create a thumbnail with Beyoncé's image and a video Title that says "my shocking interview with Bey" unless you actually did interview her. Instead, if you do want to talk about or review something, Beyoncé did be honest about it in the title (My honest review of Bey's new album) and make sure the thumbnail is appropriate and accurate.

Description - The other thing you want to include is a robust description of what your video covers. Video descriptions assist with YouTube's search and discovery system. They are a crucial source of information for YouTube's algorithm; so don't skip over this part. The copy that goes here should be meaningful to the reader and also include the same main phrases or keywords you used in the "Tags" field. This is also a great place to add extra resources, links to your website, or any other appropriate call to action.

Think mobile - As you create a description copy as well as your thumbnail, remember that most people are watching on mobile. So that image and those written words need to be pleasant to the eye if you want to attract and keep the attention of potential followers. If you're going to add words to your thumbnail, keep in mind the image will be really small for mobile users, so you want to use the least amount of words on the image to pass on your core message.

These are some of the critical things you need to do when setting up a channel, now let's talk about the essential equipment required to make you a YouTube superstar.

Do you need expensive, complicated equipment?

Absolutely not. Sure, it looks impressive when you see these YouTubers with amazing studio set-up with lots of lights, different camera angles, and what seems like an army of professionals helping them produce TV quality videos. Don't let that frazzle you in any way. I don't think anyone needs all that to begin with. I'm going to share with you what you need, whether you're working with zero budget or if you have some money to invest.

The only YouTube equipment checklist you need with or without a budget

We live in the greatest time in human history, where each of us walks around with a mini-studio where one can self-broadcast at zero cost. That's right. You can always spend money to make your equipment fancier, professional-looking, and higher quality, but don't let any of that stop you if you're starting the business with zero funds.

For those with zero budget:

All you need to start building real followers, making some good YouTube money, and having the lifestyle you've always dreamed of is:

☑ A smartphone.

☑ A laptop with editing software like iMovie (free for Mac) or Camtasia.

☑ Graphics editing software like Canva (free for all) for your thumbnails.

☑ A large window for sunlight to come through for that beautiful free lighting.

☑ A small echo-free room and some books to hold your camera so your audio can come out great, and your image will not be shakey.

These three pieces of tech, free sunlight, and some creativity with the space you have are all you need, and you can put blinders on everything else until you start seeing real results.

For those with a little budget:

You can invest as much or as little as you want. What I can assure you is that any investment made will pay high dividends. For example, within the last two years, I've invested about $2,000 in equipment and software for my YouTube channel. Within that time alone, I've made over $45,000 in ads alone. I've also made tens of thousands in affiliate sales and sponsorships.

So as you can see, making that initial investment has proven very profitable. Still, you should know, I didn't start out with the equipment. That's why only you should get to decide what equipment to buy and when. Either way, I'm going to share with you the material and tips I wish I knew when I first got started.

To get your channel looking professional and help your videos get more views, here's what you need.

☑ A good quality camera that shoots high-quality digital video.

I recommend the DSLR camera, such as the Canon 70D. This one will shoot for 30 minutes continuously, is very easy to use even for an amateur, and is friendly to the pocket.

☑ A high-quality lapel microphone.

It doesn't have to be super expensive. I suggest Lav mics because they tend to pick up less background noise in comparison to camera-mounted microphones. As a matter of fact, I use one that costs under $30 and produces really great sound. YouTube viewers might let you get away with poor lighting, but audio quality needs to be excellent; otherwise, they will all run away. Rode or Blue Yeti are a few brands you want to check out on Amazon. They have fantastic sound quality at very affordable prices, and you can get a microphone that plugs right into your smartphone or Camera.

Extra tip:

If you are planning to do lots of interviews, especially if you'll be attending conferences and events, you can hook each interviewee with their own lav mic connected to a digital recorder or use an omnidirectional handheld microphone that can also be connected to a digital recorder. And trust me, for this type of recording, you really do want to invest in a digital recorder because that's the best way to capture quality sound without background noise. This will also enable you to interview multiple people at once. I bet you're now wondering what a digital recorder is? Good. Let's talk about that next.

☑ A digital recorder.

While this is certainly only for those who are serious about producing the highest and best quality, I encourage you to consider getting one and using this along with your rode microphone. At first, even I had no idea what a digital recorder was or why I needed it. So let me save you some overwhelm and simplify it for you. This is a piece of equipment that enables you to transform any environment into a studio-like effect. Not only does it help transform any recorded sound into something crisp and studio-quality, but it also takes in more than one sound recording at a time. That means, if you inter-view someone, you can have control over the quality of both your sounds, ensuring the end consumer gets the best sound possible. I recommend getting yourself a Zoom H4N pro. It is portable, handy, and considered by many (myself included) to be the best digital recorder in the market.

☑ A tripod.

You'll need a camera or smartphone tripod, depending on your budget. Tripods help stabilize video imagery. Almost every YouTuber I know used the Amazon Basics 60-in tripod, so that's what I invested in too. There are others that are more expensive. Again, it all comes down to your budget, but this will serve as a good start.

Extra tip:

If you're going to be moving around doing vlogger videos, then I suggest you get yourself a nice hand-held tripod like the Gorillapod by JOBY. It's a sturdy tripod that is strong enough to handle a camera while still remaining super flexible, which means you can position it any way you like. I'm sure there are other options on Amazon, so do a bit of research.

☑ Video editing software.

I use Camtasia, and it has served me well for many years. It's an easy to use program, inexpensive and great for people working with a tight budget. If you can, however, I encourage you to get Adobe Premiere Pro. I am in the midst of migrating to that software as I write this book. One of the added benefits of getting Adobe Premiere Pro is you can also edit and create amazing thumbnails so you won't need any other graphics software.

☑ Teleprompter.

Ever wonder how some YouTubers seem to effortlessly flow through their content even if they are beginners? Well, there's a secret hack. It's called a teleprompter. I know a lot of people think using a teleprompter is cheating, but it's not. It is an efficient way of expressing your message, and it will save you hours of editing and filming. Check out Caddie Buddy if you're looking for something good and cost-friendly.

☑ Good lighting.

You need to have equipment that helps you light up your face or subject with no shadows. It takes more than just switching on the light to make a great video. You need an understanding of soft light and equipment that helps you pull it off whenever needed. An easy set up that many YouTubers are using is a ring light system. You can also use the traditional three-point photography set up with umbrella lights. If you opt for the umbrella lights, remember to get bulbs that are 5500k or higher.

☑ Memory card.

When it comes to getting a memory card, I say go as big as you can. I use 64 GB cards, and quite frankly, I've never reached the limit. Since they don't cost very much, I say get the biggest one your budget can handle.

☑ Grey card.

A grey card is a piece of equipment that's also essential. It helps you adjust the white balance on your camera. You may not see why this would be important to have, and that's okay, I didn't either. For a long time, I just used the default on my camera, and it seemed okay until I tested a grey card on my camera. The color quality increased exponentially. I am not saying it is a must-have, but if you care about details and color quality, definitely get yourself a grey card.

☑ Studio backdrop.

Now we are getting into the real fancy stuff. If you want to do a white background or green screen videos, you will need a studio backdrop on which you can drape a paper canvas.

Congratulations, now you have a YouTube channel, all the right equipment, and the mindset to turn this into a money-making machine. It's time to start spilling the real secrets that separate the losers from the winners on YouTube. Flip the page to the next section.

SECTION TWO: GROWING YOUR FOLLOWING FAST

3

PICKING YOUR NICHE AND TOPIC

I f you get into YouTube marketing trying to reach everyone, you'll end up reaching no one. That is one of the great marketing secrets that few newbies understand. Most of the people who are making good money on YouTube are not doing so because they started a channel for the sole purpose of making money. Instead, they are making money because they are solving a specific problem for a particular audience. Let that sink in.

In today's highly competitive marketplace where everyone is vying for attention, you need to have the right strategy in place to make your channel work. What do I mean?

In the 1970s, the average American consumer saw

around 500 ads per day. Internet and social media as we know it didn't exist, so as you can imagine, things were very different back then. That number has increased by a factor of ten since then, and we are told that the average consumer sees over 5000 ads per day. On top of that, we now have millions of blog posts published daily, over four hundred videos natively uploaded within the YouTube platform, and you think winging it will help you become a YouTube money maker?

Think again.

You've got to be able to stand out in this crowd. As fierce and competitive as it may seem, it is possible, but it requires smart thinking. Instead of trying to reach all the 30 million visitors coming into YouTube every day, focus on getting a small fraction of that audience hooked on your content. You do that by picking a topic or what we refer to as "niche" in the marketing world.

Whenever I get into a conversation with an aspiring YouTuber, he or she wants to become famous and make a lot of money, but they rarely have a clear idea of the topic they wish to specialize in.

Others argue that choosing a niche is limiting, and

they don't want to be placed in just one category because it messes with their creativity. I get it, Ann. I know you want to prove that you don't fit into any category and that you're the best at cooking, fashion, travel, and art. I know you think of yourself as a citizen of the world and would rather not focus on the fact that you're an Asian woman raised in Canada and now traveling across Europe to discover local culture and cuisine. But I can assure you unless you narrow down your topic, emphasis on that unique angle (i.e., Asian extrovert exploring European Culture), it's going to be hard for you to build a tribe of loyal followers when there are thousands of woman doing lifestyle and travel vlogs. See where I'm going with this?

To help you and your brand avoid what my client called "drowning in the YouTube Ocean of content" here's how to pick your niche and determine the main topic you will focus on at least at the beginning. Once you've decided this, we'll dive into how to identify the right audience to speak to, as well as how to attract them with compelling content.

First things first.

What is a niche?

In marketing, a niche refers to a specific group of people within a broader market that you can serve based on their narrow needs and preferences. Whenever you publish videos, you will get a lot of casual viewers who are maybe curious about your topic or are just looking for a way to pass the time. We are certainly not looking to exclude such people because, at the end of the day, we want attention. But if we only got these types of people, it wouldn't be easy to succeed. By defining and focusing on a specific niche, you're choosing to serve a very specific group of individuals, which will enable you to speak directly to them in a way that is relevant and meaningful. You're essentially saying, "I don't want to be all things to all people; I want to serve you." In so doing, you will notice your videos will rank higher, faster, and you'll start getting real engagement pretty quickly.

Choosing your niche:

Here's an interactive exercise I want us to perform. Take your YouTube journal and open a blank page. Draw three circles that all interconnect or overlap at some point. Label each circle A, B, and C. Now write "Passion" next to A. Next to B, write "Problem" and on C write "Earning Potential." If you actually drew this out, you now have what's known as "the magic zone," the point where all three overlap, and that is where you want to narrow down to. The more specific you can get with your content, the easier it will be to attract people who are very interested in that particular topic. Not only will people want to consume every content you produce, but it will also help create emotional connections within the YouTube community around that specific niche. People will start to see you as the go-to person, the expert authority on that topic. That is where real influence comes from on social media.

When choosing your niche, you'll want to start with a broad topic that you have interest in, study the channels covering this topic, and then narrow your focus to a sub-topic or group within that so you can stand out more quickly.

How I helped my client easily compete and stand out as a newbie in the travel space.

One of my clients came to me with three stale blogs and a dream of making money on YouTube. She had been blogging about fashion, travel, food, and post-graduate life. None of them were bringing in a positive return on investment, and she was at the point of giving up when a friend told her that vlogging was the easy way to make money. She was shocked when I told her otherwise. With her mindset, approach, and the fact that she was all over the place with her topics, it would be very difficult to make any money on a competitive platform like YouTube.

At first, she was very reluctant to define and focus on just one niche because she felt it was limiting her creativity. But given the fact that all her efforts had failed and this was her last straw before her parents would force her to get a real job, she took me on my word. She identified a niche within the travel space. She didn't just become a travel vlogger, she focused on being a travel vlogger for other aspiring travel vloggers who were introverted. So she narrowed it down to travel enthusiasts who wanted to start their own vlog, travel the world, and were also introverts. Her channel has become very profitable in the last twelve months, and she just reached 50.9K subscribers. On any given video, she will reach over one hundred and fifty thousand and get about 300 comments. That is the power of niching down.

Another example I can offer is let's say you are an expert in personal finance, but you stopped working to raise a family. Consider narrowing down your niche to a specific group like stay at home moms and perhaps even focusing first on how to save more money on a single income. So it could be teaching personal finance but to a particular group of people or a very specific aspect of personal finance.

But doesn't that mean I will lose everyone else?

Not at all. That is a misconception that newbies have. Choosing a niche doesn't mean you won't be able to attract other people or a broader audience. Whenever you hear someone telling you not to narrow down because it will repel other people, don't listen to them for a second. My client creates content specifically for introverted travel vloggers. Yet, her audience also includes extroverts, couples traveling the world, older couples that are looking for new experiences, and so on.

Don't be afraid to niche down. Besides, once you become seen as a trusted resource on a specific topic, and people get accustomed to your brand, you can always expand or broaden your topics a bit more. Getting back to that example of the personal-finance for stay-at-home-moms, even if you've narrowed down to taking specifically to stay-at-home-moms, you will still attract people who aren't necessarily in that demographics. You will have single moms, working moms, and all kinds of demographics showing up to consume your content because everyone wants to improve their personal finance and save more money. Narrowing down on your niche at the start doesn't limit your ability to serve other people, it helps you bring together your tribe and form a brand of loyal followers faster.

Let's go back to the YouTube journal page where you drew the three circles and dive deeper into the three circles you labeled. Please be thoughtful as you answer the questions I am about to ask.

Passion:

What are you passionate about and or interested in? Are there things on your bucket list you've always wanted to do or have been doing for years just because you have so much fun? What are your hobbies? If you notice, we tend to be passionate and interested in the things we are good at. So if you have a hard time figuring out your passion, start jotting down your skills, experience, and what you believe you're good at.

This is no time for modesty. I want you to boldly show yourself that you have talent. Think about what people generally come over and ask you about because they trust your suggestions or opinion on the matter. You might not see yourself as an expert or particularly talented. Still, I have a feeling there is something you've always done really well and enjoyed doing it. That's an important thing to remember. You've got to enjoy it. If you don't, you'll quit too soon, and the content creation process will feel more like punishment. Start thinking about the activities you've had the most experience with over the years and also what you've noticed people want to know more about. It can be as simple as knitting or as wild as mountain climbing. All that matters is that you genuinely care about this topic, and you know people already ask you about it.

If you're not sure what you're passionate about that could turn into a profitable YouTube business, I encourage you to try or learn something unique every single day for the next thirty days. By trying out new things, taking new courses, you'll eventually learn what you like and what you don't like and, more importantly, what you're good at.

What you might end up realizing is that some of the things you like doing don't really interest you long-term. This is a good thing to know before investing tons of energy and time into building a channel that will only bore you after a few months. That's when quitting happens.

Case in point, I have a friend who works as a manager for a major corporation. Six months ago, he got really enthusiastic about quitting his job and becoming his own boss doing what he "loves" and living life on his own terms. After watching me go from struggle and barely paying my bills to success and consistent income from my YouTube channel, he was totally convinced that this was the right thing to do. Of course, as a friend, I support his dream entirely, but given his employee mindset, I wanted to make sure he really understood what it was like to earn a living around a YouTube business. So I gave helped him create a strategy that would enable him to quit his job twelve months after starting his YouTube channel. The starting point of this new change, however, was for him to identify his niche, find what he's genuinely passionate about and create content for no less than three months before making any significant investments. And when I say significant investments I mean we didn't even buy a camera. We stuck to minimal equipment leveraging his iPhone, Ipad, and Mac to do all the recording, editing, and publishing. The only thing we bought was a small lav microphone.

The first two weeks seemed to go well. Once we got into the third week, however, he started slowing down. Before this, he had been convinced that photography was his passion and would casually make fun at BBQs that he would make money online faster than me if he ever committed to it. Now that he was actually doing it (shooting videos and taking pictures daily), he realized that although it had been a hobby, he enjoyed since childhood, doing it every day was quickly becoming a chore. After trying this for a month, he got back to me, saying, *"I can't see myself doing this for the rest of my life."* That insight saved him a lot of heartaches.

It's one thing to have a childhood hobby that you sometimes do and an entirely different thing creating a YouTube business out of it. So, on the one hand, you don't want to choose your niche based on income. It has to be based on something you're passionate about. On the other hand, you want to make sure that your chosen passion is something you can see yourself doing every single day for a really long time because, again, YouTube is about creating fantastic content at scale. We will dive more into the content creation part, for now, take some time to decide what topic or topics you enjoy then run them through a test to find the winning idea.

Problem:

Another way of looking at this can be - is there a demand for the topic you want to cover? If people are consuming content, buying products, and services around that topic, then the chances of having success are very high. While I do believe you can talk about anything and build a community on YouTube, not every topic will lead to income. Talking about petting unicorns, for example, is a bad idea because no one is really searching for that topic, and it will be tough to have any real monetization strategy on the back of such content. Of course, if you're just doing it for fun and don't care about demand, then go ahead, talk about whatever you want. However, this book is designed for people who actually want to have a profitable YouTube business.

A business has to be making money; otherwise, it's not really a business; therefore, focus on creating excellent content that's in demand. How? By solving a problem within your chosen niche.

An excellent place to start is by looking at other people in the same niche. This will help you identify the problems viewers are having. So try to figure out what other channels are doing to keep people engaged, how they approach the problems they solve for their audience, and see if you can find a gap or something that's missing in their approach. Then you can go and create content that fills that gap instantly, making you super valuable to your potential subscribers. You can also check comments to see if the viewers are suggesting improvements, asking questions, or the insights they offer regarding that topic.

Earning Potential:

Before you invest all your time in building out a channel-specific to a niche that you love, it's essential to educate yourself on what the market is willing to pay for.

In today's online shopping world, it's likely that regardless of the topic, people will spend money on the offer you make as long as the offer makes sense. However, I encourage you to do a little research and make sure there is competition.

Competition is a good thing. If the word competition scares you, it's time to work on your mindset. Competition means there's a demand for your product or service. There's no need for you blindly jump into a niche where no one has shown any sign of activity. While I do like the thought of pioneering, I also know that it will take you ages to monetize your YouTube channel. In short, if people aren't already doing what you want to do and making good money from it, chances are, it's not a viable business. Instead of allowing competition to scare you off, be encouraged, and take that as a sign that if you become the best and give the most value, you will have a lot of business.

YouTube's algorithms don't work like other social media platforms:

If you have already invested some time building an audience on other social platforms like Instagram, Facebook, or if you've done blogging and know a bit about the Google algorithm, you'll be surprised to know that all that knowledge won't help you much on the YouTube platform.

There is an algorithm at work on YouTube, but it works differently than other algorithms when it comes to promoting your content. YouTube serves your new videos to a small segment on your existing subscribers first. Usually, this will be the subscribers that have watched videos similar to your latest content. They place your video on the subscriber's home page and subscription feed. If you have success with that initial segment and your video gets enough clicks and engagement that the YouTube algorithm deems good enough, then your video will be distributed to a broader audience. In other words, if many of your existing subscribers click on the video, YouTube will circulate it to more subscribers and to some extent, non-subscribers who are searching for or have watched similar content. If non-subscribers also click and engage with your video, the platform will expand your reach even further enabling you to capture more attention.

When I emphasize the importance of choosing a niche and creating valuable content around that specific topic, this is the main reason for doing so. As you can see, the platform keeps bidding in your favor and getting you in front of an audience based on the data it receives that is determined by who is clicking and how much of the video they are watching. The more people click and watch, the further they push your reach. The less they take action, the less traction you get with growing your channel.

What does this mean to you and your niche?

Let's paint two scenarios here. In the first scenario, let's imagine a YouTuber with no specific niche and no clear strategy. People that subscribe to his or her channel may do so because the YouTuber's personality is pleasant, but they aren't likely to engage in most of the content he or she publishes. In such a situation, the YouTuber will release a video; the algorithm will push it out to a small segment, many of who won't click through it, and that, in turn, becomes a negative signal to YouTube. The platform will not push the content to a broader audience, which means less traction for the YouTuber, slower growth, and no business results.

Now let's imagine a YouTuber that's read through this book or has worked with me and has an identified niche with a well thought out content strategy. It's more likely that the subscribers who join this community are very interested in the subject matter, which means whenever this YouTuber publishes content, the subscribers will be attracted to the channel and engage with the content. YouTube will segment as always, more subscribers will click, which will send a positive signal to YouTube, and as a result, the content will be pushed out to a broader audience. That is why I have invested an entire chapter on picking your niche.

Another thing to keep in mind, especially for YouTubers that already have an established channel, is that switching topics will affect your views and reach. This is something I recently faced as well; so let me help you avoid this pitfall before it's too late. For example, I talk about entrepreneurship and how to work from home on my channel. Both these topics have to do with business, but they aren't necessarily the same audience. If I do a series of twelve work from home videos over two weeks, many of my new subscribers are going to be those interested in working from home ideas. If I then switch over to doing content around investing or Venture capital insights, those new subscribers are likely in that initial YouTube test group to see my investing video on their feed and may not be interested in watching.

That's not to say you won't be successful with videos in different but related topics, it's more a matter of understanding which videos to promote and how to work within that system.

Based on my experience, you can see two problems arise when you get to my level with a large enough following. First is that when new people subscribe and expect to see only specific content, they may not be interested in something else even if it's related to the same space. The other problem is that since YouTube is continuously doing a test drive whenever you publish a video, they seem to be doing a test with your most recent subscribers. YouTube wants to see if these new subscribers are going to become regular consumers or if it was just a one-time thing. Either way, the switch in focus leads to a drop in reach most of the time. While I don't mind it too much and have found ways around it, it is worth to consider creating two different channels if it makes sense for your business objectives. Of course, I am only suggesting this if you actually have a broad enough audience, and you're monetizing that first channel. Otherwise, stick to the basics and make that first channel work.

The most popular niches on YouTube:

This list is far from exhaustive, and I'm pretty sure new ones keep popping up, but just to give you an idea of what's currently profitable and popular, here are some examples.

- Gaming.
- Product Reviews.
- Tutorials.
- Food.
- Tech Videos.
- Fashion.

- Beauty.
- Travel.
- Animals.
- Humor.
- Weight loss and Healthy Living.
- Storytime videos.
- Daily Vlogs.

4

IDENTIFYING YOUR AUDIENCE

To create better content, you will need to invest some time and effort into determining whom you want to speak to. That is why I encourage all YouTubers to build an audience persona from the get-go. Personalization and customization of your content will help your channel succeed way more than a broader channel. That is because more and more Internet users, especially millennials, care about brands that personalize their marketing efforts. As such, crafting the right message for the right audience is simply a must on YouTube. The best and most cost-effective tool you can build to help you with is an audience persona document.

What is an audience persona?

An audience persona is a fictional character, usually based on real data and market research that represents a segment of your target audience. When you choose a niche, you also need to factor in that there are real humans at play. The more you can understand and speak to the needs and aspirations of those humans, the higher your chance of success with your videos. That means you need to conduct a bit of research to find out who your ideal viewer is and what they care about. There's no rule on how many audience personas you should create, but I recommend starting with 2. We take time to develop our audience personas so we can get better at knowing what they care about and what they are interested in. It also enables us to identify their challenges, needs, and desires, all of which become content ideas for us.

Questions that will help you identify your audience

1. What is this person's demographics? Think of things like where they live, their marital status, annual income, gender, age, family situation, and hobbies. This helps you paint a more personal picture of your potential subscriber.
2. What is this person's level of education? Try

to be as specific as you can here because understanding educational background helps you speak in the language that most resonates with your audience.

3. What is this person's career situation? It's important to know where your audience is currently at on his or her professional journey. Think about it, a college dropout resonates with different messages than an academic going for a Ph.D. even if you're teaching both of them about making money. Similarly, if you're creating content for someone in the prime of his or her career, then your content should reflect that. If they are looking to switch careers, then that's something you should also consider when mapping out your content. You want to think from the persona's perspective, the role they have, the challenges they are facing, and what a typical day looks like for them. All these things will enable you to produce better content that emotionally engages them.

4. What is this person's main problem or pain as it relates to your niche and the topics you cover? Think in terms of the issues your

potential subscribers are trying to solve or a hassle that's inconveniencing their lifestyle or something that's holding them back from success.

5. What is this person's aspirations or desires? This is the flip side of pain, which is equally as important for a creator to consider. Goals, desires, and aspirations are the positive things your audience wants to achieve or experience. For many successful travel vloggers on YouTube, they understand the importance of tapping into this aspect of their audience person. You want to be in a position to name it, demonstrate it, or paint a very vivid picture of that desire. It might be something personal or professional, depending on the kinds of products and services you sell. The bottom line is that you need to know what this person's end game is.

6. How does this person most enjoy learning or consuming information? You want to be creating the least amount of friction for your personas. Some people want small quick tips. Others want hour-long training videos; others prefer to see interviews and Q&A type of content. It's important to know

which content people want to see from you and how they want it delivered. The more you can match those preferences for your chosen niche, the better your videos will perform.

7. What is this person's shopping preference? We ask this question and try to answer to the best of our ability even if we are just starting out because, again, if you go after a niche and an audience that doesn't shop online or trust online education, then it's unlikely you'll make lots of money. You want to find that audience that is actively doing research and spending money in some way, shape, or form as a result of their YouTube activity. So think along the lines of do they look at reviews, ask friends and family, or something else? Do they trust social media enough to influence their purchase behavior?

Once you've gone through this exercise and answered all questions that are relevant to your niche and the business objectives you have, check out a site like Xtensio to finish building out a documented audience persona. You can also browse through some stock imagery and find a picture that you feel best represents your persona. I like to name all my personas and generally build out my audience persona document using a word document. Remember, the most important thing is to identify your ideal persona's pain/problem and his or her goals as it relates to your chosen niche. The deeper you go into this, the better. It won't happen in an hour, so give yourself enough room for research and development. Make it a regular habit to keep digging deep even outside of YouTube to discover what makes your target market tick.

5

BRANDING AND BUILDING YOUR TRIBE

W hen you think of Coca-Cola, what comes to mind?

I mean, after all, Coca-Cola is just a carbonated, sugary soft drink, right? Not quite. I'm sure you'll agree with me that Coca-Cola has become a way of life for many people globally. The company doesn't just sell soft drinks; it sells an emotional connection, a sense of belonging, and a feeling of love and happiness. That's how they are able to make 215 billion dollars a year, and that's the power of branding.

Let me prove to you how powerful this idea is. I don't particularly enjoy soft drinks, so I never buy any. But whenever I get to the Christmas season, "the holidays are coming" jingle always comes to mind. As I find myself thinking about holiday plans, meals, shopping, and family dinners, I immediately think about Coca-Cola. Every year I always end up buying a pack in my home, and you'll find me with a glass of Coke when I go for family Christmas gatherings. I know I'm not alone in this. You may think of happiness or smiling whenever someone mentions Coca-Cola. The company has done an incredible job over the years to create these emotional connections and associations in the last 130 plus years. Slogans like "holidays are coming," "always Coca-Cola," "Open Happiness," and their consistent messaging over the last one hundred years has caused all of us to be imprinted with emotional triggers that cause us to think of the company during certain seasons.

For me, it's Christmas, and I have a feeling it's from my childhood seeing Santa riding a sleigh drinking Coca-Cola as he delivered gifts (I love Santa). All of this to point out to you that building your brand is a must in 2020. Your brand isn't just about colors and logos or serving an immediate need. It should encompass deeper values, shared emotional connections, and benefits that outweigh the actual product or service.

Building a brand isn't something that can happen in a day or a week or a month. It will take time to build your brand, but you've got to start somewhere. Therefore I don't want you to get too stuck in the weeds with this topic, but I do want you to have it in the back of your mind as you continue to work on growing your YouTube channel. Building your tribe and establishing your brand can and should happen simultaneously. And while you don't really have control over the number of subscribers you get with every published video, you can at least control the image, identity, and core message that each video communicates to your new and existing subscribers.

Why is branding important?

To answer why branding is essential, we need to take a step back and understand what the term means.

According to the encyclopedia of Entrepreneur, branding is defined as the marketing practice of creating a name, symbol, or design that identifies and differentiates a product from other products. I would add to that official definition that branding is about how you make your audience feel. It's an emotional connection and trust that can only be developed over time.

When it comes to your YouTube channel, everything you choose, from the name, the colors, the channel art, your image icon, as well as how you introduce yourself all form part of your branding. The more congruent your channel, the easier it will be for people to start associating you with a particular feeling and to perceive your brand in a certain way. I wouldn't worry too much about the nitty-gritty of brand building because, as I said, it takes a long time to build a brand. How long? Think of Nike, Coca-Cola, Apple, Amazon, IBM, and Tiffany, just to name a few globally recognized brands. These companies have poured billions into their branding efforts and continue to do so. That's why we can quickly identify them. I am not expecting you to do the same or even compare yourself with any of these brands, but I always want you to think from that "big" mindset as you create and publish. Give people a reason to remember you after they're done watching your video.

A simple way to do this, especially on YouTube, is by sharing your creation story. Think about the fact that we are so drawn to Spiderman and Iron man not only because they can kick butt but also because they have unique origin stories. Consider the fact that Spiderman feels so relatable, and we instantly connect, empathize, and remember him because of how moving his creation story is. Whenever greatness is humanized and brought down closer to our grasp, we always make a strong connection. You don't need to be a superhero or get bitten by a radioactive spider to have a great creation story that helps you build your brand and attract a tribe. What you need to do is map out on your YouTube Journal what the major turning points in your life have been, then gain clarity on the core message you want people to get when they start hanging out with you. Then work backward from that point until you start to see a common philosophy or set of belief that you feel connect you with your ideal persona. Often you'll realize that the hardships, pain, or failures you've experienced are a perfect stepping-stone for establishing a brand that resonates with your ideal audience.

Another simple way to start building your brand could be in the way you dress.

Most YouTubers dress in T-shirts. What if you decided to innovate and wear something that stands out like James Bond? Of course, your dress style needs to be authentic to you because if you fake it, people will figure it out sooner rather than later, and it will destroy your brand equity. Authenticity in the way you speak, how you dress, and the background you choose for your videos are simple things you can do to start creating resonance and demonstrating shared values with your growing tribe. When you do your best to show more of who you really are and what you believe about yourself, people will notice that difference. Which leads me to my next point.

What you can do now when it comes to branding is to find your differentiator.

There is something unique about how we do anything. No two snowflakes are alike, did you know that? Even your fingerprints are unique, which means you can talk about the same topic as another YouTube influencer and still brand yourself as completely different. To do so, you must know and leverage your uniqueness.

What makes you different?

Is it your fashion taste, your world-view, something in your background, a talent you possess, a physical attribute? Spend some time thinking about this and grab that YouTube journal we've been using so far to list down anything that comes to mind.

Exercises to help you find your differentiator.

1. Ask your friends and family members why they like hanging out with you and what they remember most about you. Is there a statement they've noticed you like repeating?
2. What is your outlook on life?
3. What is your big "why"?
4. What are your crazy ideas?
5. What ideas do you want your business to represent?
6. How can you change the current rules of the games in your chosen niche?
7. What's missing or what are people scared to talk about in your chosen niche?
8. What are the most apparent benefits people will get from watching your channel or using your products/services?
9. What do you think is the most memorable thing about you?
10. What is your vision for this YouTube channel? What's your vision for your life?
11. How do you want people to think and feel when they spend time on your channel or use your product/service?

To start developing your brand, here's a simple equation I want you to make equal.

Your self-impression = how people perceive you.

7 steps to organically start building your tribe fast on YouTube:

When you consider the fact that on other social media platforms, people don't invest as much time as they do on YouTube, it should encourage you to go all-in with your content strategy. Quicksprout shared an infographic earlier this year that showed the average daily time spent on YouTube is 40 minutes. Compare that with Facebook's 35minutes, Snapchat's 25minutes, Instagram 15minutes, and Twitter's 1-minute average, and it makes all the effort you'll put in worthwhile. People love to binge-watch videos on YouTube, which means there's a massive opportunity for you to grow a loyal tribe of subscribers. In an upcoming section, we spend more time going through in-depth strategies that will enable you to build your channel fast within the next twelve months. Before jumping into that section, here are a few tactics I want you to start implementing.

Step one: Personalize your videos.

This sounds counterintuitive when you're just starting out, but I can assure you, it will help you capture the attention of a viewer faster than trying to be broad. When you're looking to build a powerful tribe of people who will subscribe, not just watch your video, I have found that the more personalized my video is, the better it performs. For example, because I target more of my local area, I usually begin at least one video each week, specifically talking to individuals in my local area. I give an anecdote or my thoughts on something that only people who are from here or currently live here would get. I've realized those videos have the highest engagement.

I also noticed a YouTuber in the relationships niche doing the same. She's grown exponentially within the last six months. If you click her videos, you will see she regularly addresses men (her niche is helping a man attract a woman) from Florida, where she lives. And when you look at the hundreds of comments she's getting, people tend to say that they are definitely going to stay tuned in because she's from their hometown as well. That is the power of personalization.

It's something many rappers and singers understanding very well. They always push for local influence before attempting to take on the world. Perhaps that's something you want to play with. It's easier for someone who lives in your hometown to hit subscribe when you specifically address them and solve a problem in your video because it creates an instant connection.

Step two: Decide on a consistent publishing schedule.

To help potential subscribers join your tribe, you want to show them that you're the reliable go-to person for that topic. Then create an expectation within them by publishing content in a consistent matter, almost creating a routine in their minds so that they get used to coming in to see what's new whenever they are on YouTube on that particular day or days. If, like me, you have two topics that are from the same niche but slightly varying in angle, explicitly let your audience know when to expect which topic.

I shared this tactic with a client who, similar to me, focuses on two topics within the same market. The overarching similarity is money, but sometimes he teaches on getting out of debt, and other times, he teaches investing. Instead of creating different channels, he begins his "getting out of debt" videos by letting the viewer know that every Tuesday, he published fresh content on the topic. Then with his investing video, which comes out on Fridays, he also lets them know that this particular topic only happens on his Friday show. He also has identifiable playlists, which make it easy for a new or returning subscriber to navigate. There are other advanced hacks he's using, which I will be sharing with you once we get to optimize your channel. Still, I hope this has sparked your creativity so you can find smart ways of ensuring your scheduling remains consistent for your viewers.

Step three: Create a binge-worthy series-based content.

Something very few YouTubers take the time to think about is their end consumer behavior. You are assured of success if you can keep your pulse on what consumers want and how they like to consume things. The current trend is the binge-watching effect, which means making individual stand-alone videos is a poor strategy when you're trying to grow your channel fast. Think of Netflix, Amazon Prime, and other platforms that have come up completely disrupting television. The reason they do so well is that we are in an era where people want to choose what they watch and for how long.

The old mentality that's failing many YouTubers is creating one viral video that blows up and makes them an overnight celebrity. This isn't an approach I encourage my clients and students to take because it hardly ever delivers real results. Instead, I want you to focus on creating amazing videos, one leading right into the next. That way, if a potential subscriber finds one of your videos, they will get hooked on your immediately because there will be a series of videos to take them on that journey of getting to know, like, and trust you while simultaneously getting value.

Step four: Start implementing the growth formula

To do this, you need to look at the search volume that matches the size of your channels. So if you're a brand new channel, it's not a good idea to pick a topic that has too high a volume. At least not in the beginning when you're trying to capture the attention of your first 1000 subscribers. A better to approach this when starting from scratch is to look for search volume that is mid-level to a low level within that narrowed down niche of your broader well-researched topic. When you can find a niche in that more general topic that has 1000 search volume and with less than 5000 results popping up, your chances of ranking really fast and being found by potential subscribers exponentially rises.

Step five: Research your peers

In other words, do a bit of stalking on the channels that are serving the same audience you want to attract. Check to see the videos that are already ranking for the topic you want to make a video around and investigate these two metrics: How many views did they get and over what time period? In this context, you want to find videos that have a higher view count over a shorter period. You also want to see a higher number of views in relation to the subscriber count. For example, if someone has 90 subscribers and a million views on a video, that means that, the video is getting picked up in search and being suggested by the algorithms a lot. It's a popular topic with a lot of demand, so creating your better version of the same topic is a really great way to grow your subscriber count fast.

Step six: Add a subscriber pop-up link

Before you can take full advantage of this tactic, I want you to make sure your channel is verified.

Another thing that is required for this step to work is you will need to secure your custom URL. A subscriber pop-link is formatted with your youtube.com/subscription_center?add_user=(YOU-RUSERNAME). Once you have obtained your custom URL and verified your account, you'll have the ability to add fill in your username after that equal sign. The main benefit and purpose of creating this pop-up link is to make it easier for you to share your YouTube channel on all your other social platforms and email communications. You can easily send it out to friends and family as well. When they click on that particular link, your YouTube channel pops up with a pop-up box that encourages them to subscribe immediately before they even watch any of your content. I also encourage you to add this link to every video description.

Step seven: Make great content

It's so simple even children get it! Perhaps that's why they are making lots of money on YouTube. I sometimes come across these channels where they say, "sub for sub," and I just don't get it. I am totally confused as to why I would subscribe to your channel just for the sake of it when your content sucks. Please stay away from those types of hacks and tactics; they will only hurt your brand and bank account.

Instead, I want you to put all your energy into making great content. I don't mean "okay" or "good enough." I want great content. If you struggle with quantity, then focus first on quality until you get the hang of things, then ideally do both. When I first got serious about growing my channel, I was only releasing fresh content once a week because it was more important for me to create consistency and quality. Then after building momentum, I started doing twice a week, and now I'm up to six times a week.

To produce great content, you must figure out what people want. Remember the audience persona we created? That's an excellent starting point. Now that you know whom your ideal audience is - go out there and find them! If you're starting from scratch and have no audience or network to leverage, use the information you find on your competitor's channel. The videos that get the most engagement, the problems the community shares, etc. are all fantastic sources of content. Whatever you do, don't just guess. Craft content that is driven by data you've gathered from the marketplace.

The first golden rule of YouTube:

You need to build relationships within the community, so even as you deploy these tactics, remember the first golden rule of YouTube is to engage and participate within the community actively (that means every day). Remember one of the mistakes I shared that newbies make? They forget to respond to the comments that people leave on their channel. You must never do that. I also want to encourage you to be generous with your comments on channels that have the audience you wish to attract.

When I was growing my channel, I invested an hour each day solely on responding to comments, chiming in on conversations, asking and answering questions on the channels that already had people I wanted to associate with. YouTube is a social media platform. If you're going to be a highly paid YouTuber, you must become social, engaging, and generous within the community. Be generous with your knowledge and get involved in the communities of these like-minded channels. But I also want you to think beyond just the YouTube community. A quick story will help elaborate on what I mean better than dry statements.

Karey and I started working together on his

YouTube channel about two months ago. He had literally five subscribers. We obviously took him through my program and strategy. We applied everything I've shared with you so far, and one extra thing we did when it came to being an active community member is I asked him to spend an hour within YouTube interacting with like-minded channels and thirty minutes outside interacting with like-minded groups within Facebook and using Quora. I will be talking more about these advanced strategies in the optimizing section, but in summary, he's been able to reach 500 subscribers within the 8-week period we've been working together purely based on this golden rule of being an active member. You must be willing to put in the work, to be social and generous with your knowledge if you want your tribe to grow fast. A neat trick we've used with Karey includes him creating high-value content answering questions he's picked up on his Facebook groups and Quora (the ones that had a lot of attention). Then after publishing it on YouTube, he shares it on Facebook and helps a member of the group out. No selling, no gimmicks, just answering that question or solving that problem as best as he can and demonstrating that he's an expert within his niche. The result has been an increased number of high-quality subscribers. See how simple this can be? It doesn't have to be complicated, but it does require commitment, dedication, and authenticity. That one little move can already bring you significant growth if you log into your Facebook or Instagram now and find people you can genuinely help.

It's time to get a little more advanced with your YouTube strategy. Before we do, let's go over what you need to do now.

6

ADVANCED YOUTUBE STRATEGY FOR GROWING YOU AUDIENCE FAST

There's one advanced strategy that I want to share with you before moving to the next section, which can help you fast track your channel growth. It's called Adwords for video.

Did you know you could pay to promote your videos and your channel using a tool called Adwords for video? Many YouTubers are going from zero to 100,000 subscribers in less than twelve months, and it's mainly because they used this advanced technique. Of course, part of being able to make this happen requires you to have a budget. So if you are fortunate enough to set aside a little marketing budget, this is something worth implementing. But if you can barely rub two pennies together at this point and all you've got is your time and determination, then this strategy won't apply for you just yet. You can choose to skip over to the next chapter until you're good and ready to invest a little cash into your YouTube marketing. By continuing to read this chapter, I am going to assume you want to take advantage of Adwords for video, so let me know you a simple way of getting the most out of your hard-earned money.

With Adwords for video, you will easily reach an engaged audience who might not have known that your channel even exists. It is the fastest way to accelerate your channel's growth. Before you consider investing and paying money to grow your channel make sure you've gone through all the strategies, hacks, and tactics that I have outlined in this book. It's not enough to have money to invest. If your videos aren't great, spending money on Adwords for video will not yield the results you desire.

Steps for using Adwords for Video successfully

Step one: Create a really great video ad.

On YouTube, your ads can appear before a video

starts, next to a video on the watch page, on YouTube search results, or on the YouTube home-page. When shooting your video ad, make sure it's compelling, concise, and do your best to show (not tell) what your channel is all about as this will help viewers understand whether to subscribe or not. The other thing you need to do is to get to the point and have a clear call to action.

Focus on hooking viewers right from the start and make the video as long as it needs to be in order for you to pass on the clear, compelling message that will get your potential subscribers to want to visit your channel and subscribe.

I would also encourage you to create two or three variations of your ad and test them against the audience you want to attract so you can discern what works best for them. The numbers don't lie. Which-ever ad performs best will inform you of the type of content your audience wants to watch.

Step Two: Target your ideal audience

We already went into detail about the importance of identifying your perfect audience. Even if you're starting from zero, it's good to do a little research and make an educated guess because if you try to reach everyone, you'll end up with no audience or business results. Adwords for video makes it possible for you to target audiences that are passionate about a specific topic such as cooking enthusiasts or target channels or videos focused on one particular topic. You can also choose to show your ads on specific channels that might have an audience similar to yours. And you can even target your audience (for example, viewers who have watched your videos but aren't yet subscribed).

So you want to make sure you feel like you really know these four things. Who (based on the niche you've chosen this can include their interests, age group, demographics, etc.), What (choose the video or channel on which you want your ads to be shown), Where (this can include the country, region or city), When (If you have a limited budget you can pace the delivery of your ads throughout the day.)

Step Three: Use YouTube specific-ad formats

It's best to use the ad formats that are known to perform best on the platform because of their interactive elements. The more interactive they are, the more viewers will be encouraged to engage further with your content and convert. The most recommended are TrueView Discovery, TrueView In-Stream, and Bumper Ads.

TrueView Discovery - this ad appears next to related YouTube videos on YouTube search results, or on the YouTube desktop and mobile homepage. You only pay when a viewer clicks on your ad and begins watching your video. This is a great ad format to use if you want to reach specific people who are browsing or searching for specific videos in those moments of discovery.

TrueView In-Stream - this ad immediately immerses viewers into your content. After 5 seconds, they have the option to keep watching if they like what they see or to hit the skip button. The best part about this ad format is you pay when a viewer watches 30 seconds (or the whole video if shorter) or if the viewer interacts with your ad. This ad format is best when you want your video ad to appear before during, or after other videos on YouTube.

Bumper Ads - this ad is 6 seconds or shorter and plays before, during, or after another video. The best part about this ad format is that viewers cannot skip over it, so you literally have six seconds of uninterrupted attention to make your potential subscriber discover your awesome channel. For this ad format, you pay per CPM (each time your ad is served 1,000 times). If you know you've got a short, powerful, memorable message and would like to reach a broader audience with a hook that will have them running to your channel, then I highly recommend testing this ad format.

Best practices for growing your following fast using Adwords for video

Take the time to apply a strategy that matches your goals.

What is your primary objective? Never start a campaign without clearly defined goals and objectives. The reason many YouTubers attempt this paid strategy and fail is that they skip this part. You must know precisely what you want to achieve and define clear KPIs to help you track whether you're moving in the right direction or not. Otherwise, you might be dead in the water and not know it. I don't particularly think an end goal of having more followers is worthy enough to invest money on a paid strategy, so be sure to have a real business goal that can be linked to increased return on investment. Some of the goals you can choose to set include but aren't limited to growing your subscribers, expanding your reach from local to global, attracting new viewers, promoting a launch, selling merchandise, etc. Take some time to set S.M.A.R.T goals with your end game in mind. Then implement the rest of these suggested best practices before launching that campaign.

Leverage your best performing content.

Once you've started populating your channel with excellent content, when you spot one that is organically performing well, that might be a great time to invest a small budget to reach a broader audience. Build an ad that incorporates clips or concepts from your best performing video.

Tell your story.

This may not easily apply to bumper ads unless you are super creative, but for all the other ad formats, I strongly encourage you to use storytelling. Be compelling and always share a narrative that you know your audience cares about.

Provide clear next steps.

Be very concise with your call to actions when investing in paid ads strategies. Be creative with your call to action. For example, you can add a call-to-action overlay, which appears as soon as the video begins to play and can be closed by the viewers. If the viewer clicks, they're redirected to the channel your define. Always make sure to direct your viewer to take a specific action and verbalizing what you want them to do now i.e., "click anywhere on this screen to subscribe to my channel now."

Play with interactive elements.

Aside from the call-to-action overlay that I just mentioned above, YouTube also gives you additional elements that can deepen the engagement your viewer has with your video. Be smart about how you utilize them because if you overdo it, then it's just going to be a turn-off. Consider using cards and tease something (another video or playlist) for a few seconds. If you are using the TrueView In-Stream ad, you can have a companion banner that comes in the form of a clickable thumbnail. This is a great way to guide viewers to take action and "watch more" or "subscribe." Again, let me emphasize the importance of making it relevant, compelling, and tasteful. Don't spam your video with too many CTAs as that might distract your viewer and irritate them.

Recap of action steps for this section:

- Write out on your YouTube journal a list of things you are passionate about. Things you enjoy doing, hobbies you've had since childhood, as well as your bucket list. List the topics you love talking about and researching.

- Name your skills, talents, and experience. Next, I want you to start identifying problems that you can solve as it related to your experience and skillset.

- Do some research to find out if people are paying money to solve the problems you just identified. Come up with topics around that problem and drill it down to one or two levels. Narrow down some more on the topic that thrills you most.

- Identify the persona that would be most interested in that topic. Go deep into this exercise with the questions I shared and create a document that enables you to picture him or her clearly.

- Craft a story around this persona in a way that you feel they would most enjoy. Now that you know who they are, what they do, their aspirations, and pain points as well as what they do, what is the best content you can publish to bring them most value?

Remember, this is an initial picture and must be continually developed as your channel grows, and more data comes in through your Analytics tools.

- Work on identifying your uniqueness and use it to establish your brand differentiator. Figure out what your deeply held beliefs are and decide which you want to use as shared beliefs to bring together your tribe. Using your creation story, pivotal moments in your life experience, and how you carry yourself - do your best to communicate these beliefs and your philosophy in life.
- Implement most, if not all, of the steps I have outlined to grow your tribe fast.
- Find no less than ten channels that currently serve your niche and watch some of their videos for some inspiration on branding elements and more content ideas.
- Join no less than ten groups on Facebook and dedicate at least an hour to proactively get involved in the community within and outside of YouTube. Find questions or problems you can solve, create fantastic content, and share within these groups.
- If you have the budget, leveraged YouTube

ads for video to fast track your channel's growth. Your budget can be as little or as much as you decide just make sure to have high value content before implementing this advanced hack.

SECTION THREE: OPTIMIZING YOUR YOUTUBE

7

THE TWO SOURCES OF TRAFFIC YOU NEED TO HACK FOR FAST GROWTH

In this section, we are diving into the secrets that most YouTubers don't want you to know. Given the investment you've made in acquiring this book and the commitment you're demonstrating by reading and implementing everything you learn, I believe it's only fair that I share with you strategies that will exponentially grow your YouTube channel and turn you into a superstar in no time. This chapter is one of my favorites. As I sit down to type out the next couple of paragraphs, I'm getting really excited because I know these are some of the techniques that have helped my clients and students accomplish in a few weeks what took me years to master. Are you excited and ready, as well?

Good.

Fact: The only way for you to go from zero to hero real quick is by identifying the best sources of traffic and maximizing on them.

I can assure you that as a beginner or if you're someone struggling to grow an audience after months of publishing, the best way to get momentum and build your channel is by leveraging these two sources of traffic - Search and Suggestion. Ranking on YouTube platform and Google is both an art and a science. There's no guesswork involved. I want to show you the science of ranking quickly.

What is Search?

Search is when someone goes on the YouTube search bar (sometimes Google search bar), and they type in a key phrase or keyword. Usually in the form of how-to, best of, etc. You get the gist, right? The nature of YouTube is that consumers start their experience by typing something on the search bar, after which the feed populates with relevant search results. Those that are fortunate enough to rank on the first page naturally get the most traffic. Your job is to figure out how to rank as high as possible on that search results feed.

What is Suggestion?

YouTube suggestion is what we all get on the sidebar or on your homepage feed as recommended or suggested videos. Again, what you want is to for your video to show up on the feed of your Ideal Client. The more engagement your videos and channel get, the more you will show up as a suggested video for other viewers on the platform. YouTube algorithm has complete control over this, but there are a few things you can do to influence your ability to show up.

One of the benefits you get to enjoy now is that I will walk you through real-life examples and exact tactics you can pull off to start showing up on both search and suggestions. To do this, I want to show you step by step how you can build enough authority and engagement to start showing up high on search and to get added in the suggestions sidebar.

First, I want you to find the gaps in your niche and fill them.

By this, I mean you need to research again and find what's missing between search volume and search results in the topic you want to rank for.

Dr. Ruben is an excellent example of how one can go from zero to ranking on the first page of YouTube. Dr. Ruben started with zero subscribers and zero views on his videos. Within three weeks, he was already getting over two hundred views on his videos.

How is he doing this? Simple. He's applied the same strategies I'm sharing with you throughout this book. Dr. Ruben identified his niche market. He chose the topic of "managing emotions under pressure," which gets a volume of 110 per month. For someone starting out, anything between 100 - 1000 is ideal because you can easily rank for it. In terms of competition, there are 40.7k videos in search results, which is also very good because it means he's not competing against millions of videos. By finding the gap and filling it with fantastic high-value content, he's been able to rank on the first page of YouTube in just a matter of weeks. You can start to experience the same kind of growth and exposure in the next few weeks if you apply the same strategy.

Second, I want you to experiment with traffic hacking to get you into the suggested video sidebar.

Traffic hacking is a common term you will hear with prominent vloggers, YouTubers, family channels, and entertainment channels. A lot of channels will work together to make this effective, but with a little creativity, you can pull it off even on your own. All you need is to find the right headline to traffic hack. Here's how to go about it. Find the most popular video in your niche with lots of views. Use the same headline title and make your unique version of it.

The only metric YouTube Cares About That You Should Care About Too:

Here's a trick question for you. Do you know what the single most important metric on YouTube is?

If you answered the number of subscribers, views, likes, shares, or any of those usual vanity metrics, you'd be wrong! Let me demonstrate the right answer with an example.

Suppose you made a video that is two minutes long. It got one hundred views, and people watched it all the way to the end (100%). You'd have two hundred minutes in total. Now let's change things up and assume you made a video that's ten minutes long. It got fifty views (half of the views of the first example), and people watched only fifty percent of the video. You'd have two hundred and fifty minutes in total. That's 25% more in the second example than the first. According to YouTube, the second example is better because it implies more time spent on YouTube with more time to show ads and build revenue. YouTube has a word for this known as - Watch time. Every single second a user spends time watching your content on YouTube earns you credit. Granted, this credit is microscopic and takes a while to pile on as it grinds its way through the algorithm and other variables you and I have no control over. But that doesn't change the fact that if you want to win on YouTube, you need to play the platform.

In the words of the YouTube team, "We use watch time as a metric in our algorithm for suggesting videos. The algorithm prioritizes videos that lead to longer overall watch time or viewing sessions, rather than videos that get more clicks." So if you've been playing the game of obsessing over likes, shares, subscriber count, and channel size, I encourage you to refocus your energy. I'm not saying those metrics don't matter because they do. However, the main game on YouTube is to increase watch time and get people to consume as much of your video as possible. To do this, the quality of the video needs to be epic so that you can drive more retention and get people hooked on you longer. It might seem like it's a game of quantity over quality when you first learn about watch time. The truth is, you need both quality and quantity to win the YouTube game. That is the frame of mind you need before hitting that record button.

Insider hack:

Now that you understand the importance of watch time, I want to share with you a simple hack few YouTubers know about that can help increase your watch time. By optimizing your video titles, descriptions, and doing significant research on your keywords, you can be able to accumulate watch time in this ingenious way. For example, let's assume you've created epic content around the super bowl and optimized it as suggested in this book, which then leads you to rank on search. When a viewer clicks on your video, watches it, and then clicks on suggested videos, even if that next video isn't yours, you still get rewarded with credits because it was your video that drew them in and facilitated the retention of the viewer.

The more this viewer is in session, the more you get rewarded. It is known as session watch time, and the brilliance of following the advanced strategies shared in this book is that you will naturally start to generate both watch time and session watch time. Starting to see how simple it is to become a real money-maker on YouTube? Good. Let's talk about optimizing the content so you can actually get people hooked and increase watch time.

8

HOW TO MAKE YOUTUBE VIDEOS THE RIGHT WAY

If you're wondering if there's a wrong way to make videos, the answer is, unfortunately, yes! And I know this because, in the beginning, I was making this same mistake. When I first started using YouTube, it was more like a hosting platform for my blog, so the videos were obviously not YouTube friendly. Then I got that moment where a little attention got sent my way thanks to the great content I had created, and my thirst to conquer YouTube exponentially grew. I finally got the validation that I needed to go all in. Through trial and error (mostly error), I started making videos that people seemed to enjoy. As I educated myself more, it eventually got to the point where I invested in a mentor who taught me how to actually do things right. But don't be fooled, my earlier videos did suck because I just wasn't making them the right way. To help you avoid the same frustration and possible future embarrassment (what I have to go through anytime someone scrolls all the way down to my videos from years ago), here's what I want you to start doing.

The Teaser:

I want you to have a teaser at the beginning of every video. This will help people know why they should invest their time and attention on you. It will keep them hooked and signal to YouTube that your content is good and therefore deserves more attention. The game on YouTube is retention. The more you can have people watching all the way to the end, the better your channel will perform.

The Engagement:

Next, engage your audience. Give people what they want and make sure you are speaking about what you know really well. The more of an expert you feel on that topic, the better. People need to feel like they can't get access to this content anywhere else. In other words, share things that only you can share and do it sequentially. What I mean is I want you to streamline the actual content in story form so that people feel like they have to tune in for the entire thing to get the desired result.

So whether that's insider secrets that you have, a behind-the-scenes, a step-by-step tutorial, or an embarrassing moment that happened to you on stage do you best to have that meaty section of your video streamlined.

The Call to action:

Now that you've nailed that part, it's time to think about your call to action for every video. If you don't thoughtfully craft a call to action, your audience will quickly forget they ever watched you even if they loved your content. There are millions of videos on YouTube if you want people to keep coming back to you, once you deliver amazing content that engages them - ask them to take action. It can be a soft call to action that keeps them within your YouTube channel or a hard call to action that directs them to something outside of YouTube. To increase the like-lihood of getting YouTube algorithms to work in your favor and push out your video to more people, always end your video with an engagement call to action. What this means is that you ask your video to like, share, and comment on the video if they enjoyed consuming it. By taking one or all of these actions, a signal is sent to YouTube that implies your content is good and deserves to be seen by more consumers seeking similar content.

When just starting out, I encourage you to have the engagement call to action on every video. Then pick and choose which videos best fit for the hard call to actions that drive people to your website or other social platforms.

The right way to structure your YouTube videos

Many YouTubers fall short at this level of the game because they tend to think that all it takes is just setting up the channel, creating the videos and uploading them. Unfortunately, they are wrong. That is only part of the key to success if you want to make real money on YouTube. The details and the optimization is the key ingredient that will result in a channel that makes money and one that doesn't. So in this section, we focus on more advanced strategies and tactics. We focus on the details that take your video from okay or good enough to amazing. And we don't need fancy equipment to do it, just a lot of hustle and the right ideas. The first right idea is taking the time to create a template structure for your videos so they can have a harmonious feel as one watches one video after the next. By creating a structure for your videos, you naturally build interest and engagement, creates a feeling of consistency and familiarity, which helps retain the attention of your audience. As we said before, retention is the name of the game. The more people get glued to your videos, the higher the rank, the more views, and subscribers you will get.

Let's take a look at some key elements to incorporate into your structure for your video to come across more natural, engaging, and fun to watch.

Intro:

This takes up the first few seconds to a minute of your video. It is your chance to tell viewers what's about to happen and capture their attention. This is the crucial step that determines whether people will continue watching your content or not. Be very clear about what's in it for them. Explain who you are and why they should listen to you in as few words as possible. Walk them through what they can expect if they stick with you till the end.

Hook:

Transition from the intro into the main content with a compelling hook. A hook in storytelling is used to tease the audience, so they get curious, excited, and eager to consume the entire content. In the YouTube language, a hook is often referred to as a teaser. Once you give a compelling one, shift right into the meat of the video content. On Youtube, you want your hook to grab the viewer's attention right off the bat and make them want to stay tuned in. The hook is vital because it is the difference between success and failure for your video.

For example, let's say I'm doing a video on traveling around Spain; I would probably start my video with the most epic moment of my travel and working backward to tell the story of how I got to that moment. In so doing, people will know something exciting is coming, and I will be leading them all the way to that moment by the end of the video. Makes sense?

Main content:

Imagine for a moment walking into a coffee shop, ordering a sandwich, and then getting only two pieces of bread with no meat in between! Would you ever go back? That's pretty much the same awful experience your potential subscribers would have if you didn't do an excellent job with this piece of your video content. Be generous with the meat!

The sooner you can get into the meat of your video, the more people are going to be engaged with your content and watch all the way through. If it's blog-style content, make sure you jam-pack it with relevant teaching points and stories. If you're doing a tutorial, make sure you take your audience step-by-step to the final outcome.

Insider hack:

Something cool you can integrate into your main content section is to pause halfway through the meaty part of your video and ask a relevant question to encourage your audience to comment and engage with you. Make sure your question is straightforward, super relevant to the topic at hand and tell people how you want them to respond. For example, going back to my earlier case of traveling across Spain, I would get into the meat of my video, share my story with some cool teaching lessons, and at some point, I would pause and ask, "Is Spain at the top of your bucket list? If it is comment below or share which country is at the top of your bucket list." See how I directed the kind of engagement I want to have? Don't over-complicate this. The simpler it is for the viewer, the higher the chances you will get lots of participation.

Outro

This is the final piece of your video. When building up your YouTube channel, you really don't want to get into summarizing the entire video and what people learned. In other words, having a conclusion for your video is actually not good for your channel because if you give people closure, they are more likely to walk away as soon as your video's done. Instead, what you want (again going back to that binge-watching effect) is to make your outro fast, more focused on building engagement by inserting another call to action and also introducing any related videos you have that your audience will benefit from.

Here you want to remember to ask for engagement (like, share, comment) invite them to subscribe and whenever possible, ask a yes or no question in the end. Verbally ask the question and also include a card if possible.

When thinking about your outro, bring to mind what you want from your audience. What do you want them to do next? What would be a mutually beneficial action they can take? Plan your outro from that point of view.

Do you need a video script?

Most people will give a hard yes or no answer to this question, but the truth is, it depends on your personality, the kind of brand you have, and your business objectives.

The truth is, boring YouTube videos are repetitive, dull, unstructured, and the person talks at their audience. They often don't have a script or structure. Great YouTube videos tend to have a flow, and it feels like the person is speaking to a buddy over a beer or a girlfriend over coffee. But it is done in a natural yet carefully planned out manner. And yes, most of the time, it is scripted.

Many YouTubers are against scripting because they feel like it makes them less natural and relatable. As long as you know how to make your video feel like a well thought out dialogue instead of a confusing monologue, it doesn't really matter whether you use a script or not. I started out using a script, and to this day, I still take some time to write in bullet list what I want to share on the video.

If you don't feel like using a script, consider having a rough outline of your structure with bullet points of what you wish to cover. That will ensure you don't stray, become too repetitive, or fall into rabbit holes.

If you would like to use a script, make sure to write it the same way you naturally speak. I also recommend practicing it a few times before recording the final video to avoid squinting while on camera.

9

SIMPLE VIDEO EDITING TRICKS

Aside from shooting the video, the right way the other hurdle to overcome is editing the video. Many YouTubers get really frustrated and derailed by this particular task, so I want to share with you some tips that can make even a newbie creator look like a professional.

Editing your video can be very time-consuming, and it probably will be in the beginning. Eventually, as you get the hang of it, things will get easier. Mostly because you'll learn how to use your software. Good editing can turn even the most camera-shy person into a character people enjoy watching, and of course, that's what we want. The more appealing you are, the longer people will watch your video.

Unlike blogging or podcasting, the additional work that video editing requires creates a lot of friction for beginners, which can be a good thing as it limits your competition on the platform. Most will quit, so if you can find a way to keep going and make yourself better at editing your videos, the rewards that await you will be worthwhile. But make no mistake; you won't master this in a day, a week or a month. It will take time to become proficient even if you buy the best software unless you already have formal education on filming. Those first couple of dozen videos are going to be a grind, and you might even be tempted to throw in the towel. I urge you not to give up! Once you set up a process and create a routine for editing your videos, it is going to become a more natural experience. You'll be able to do it in a matter of minutes instead of days.

Tips and Tricks For The Editing Process

This chapter will not get into the nitty-gritty of editing or working with various software. Every software comes with its own learning curve, and most will offer tutorials to help you get started, so I recommend learning those editing details from your software provider. The real step-by-step of using any editing software can best be learned through tutorials, so what I am attempting to do here is give you some easy tricks that I've picked up along the way that you can apply in addition to the basics you learn from the tutorial. I hope that by incorporating this, you can save time and effort.

Before we get started on the actual tricks, it's worth talking about the software you chose for your editing process. There are free packages that you can use like Openshot and Blender, and trust me I started off trying to find the cheapest (or free) software that could work for me. Almost all fell short on the features needed to produce a quality video. Most will upsell you into their premium features anyways, so in the end, after falling for the same allure of free, my best advice is to go for something that actually works for you even if it has an upfront fee. I use Camtasia after trying Adobe Premiere Pro and Final Cut Pro. All three are amazing, but I settled for Camtasia simply because I find it easier to use. If possible, do some research on all three before settling for the one that best suits your personal taste.

Time-saving tips and tricks for beginners

Start by uploading all your video and audio files into the editor. If you run into some error check to ensure your file format works with that particular software. Sometimes, you might need to convert the file into a different format before the software can accept it. For example, Camtasia doesn't work with .mov files (I learned this the hard way). So to upload the files after shooting them with my camera, I actually need to convert them into an mp4 file. You'll also need to upload all your graphics, any backgrounds you'd like to add to the video, etc.

Remember the previous chapter where I recommended scripting your videos? Well if you do follow that approach then this stage becomes less of a hassle because during the scripting process you already create a mental picture of how the video will be, what additional graphics you'll add to emphasize specific talking points and (here comes the first cool trick), you can already place notes in the areas of the video where graphics and texts will be placed. That makes the pre-production process smoother and faster.

Another neat trick is to create a template in something like Canva that you know you'll regularly use to brand your videos and then place them in a library on the editing software. We want to make sure that graphics like "subscribe" or your end screen are congruent from day one and that you don't have to keep remaking them each time you work on a new video.

One of the most critical aspects of the editing process is splicing clips together so that the video can have a continuous flow. Let's face it, getting through an entire video without mistakes, glitches or mispronunciations is almost impossible when just starting out. So give yourself permission to screw up and cut it out. You also want to cut out the parts where you use too much filler words or awkwardly go silent, trying to remember what you want to say. Having a starting point on the floor where you end and begin each clip will help, but you'll never line things up perfectly. If all you do is splice up the video, it will end up looking awkward to the eye because your body position will be different from one second to the next. I'm sure you've seen videos that have that awkwardness, and you can't quite put your finger on it. Still, your brain automatically disqualifies it as unappealing. I want to make sure you don't have that unattractive effect with your viewers, which means we need to create a "jump cut" in the video.

If you look closely at any recorded video from

movies to Television series as well as commercials, you'll see a jump cut. What is a jump cut? It's when a person continues speaking through two clips, but the camera angle or video zoom changes. When done right, it usually looks as though this is done for emphasis on what the person is saying or cinematography, but frequently (especially with YouTubers), it's done to splice those two clips together in a professional and appealing way. See where I'm going with this? If yes, then here are a few creative tricks for making your own jump cuts.

Zoom in and cut. What I mean by this is you can zoom in the second clip 10% to 20% and then cut the second clip right to the beginning of the first word. Next, I want you to increase the video image size to that clip do that you take the bigger portion of the screen. The result is the video jumps from your first clip into the second with a quick close-up. This is the most common jump cut trick that pro YouTubers are using to make their videos look super high quality.

Use graphics. Graphics are a quick and easy way to cover up clip splicing, especially if you don't feel too confident with the software. Simply add a quick plain background with notes for a definition or some b-roll, and your video will still have that polished, high-quality look.

Use a second camera. Set the camera at a 45-degree angle while filming. That way, you don't need to work with two clips from the same camera roll. Instead, you can use a clip from this second camera for the sections that require a jump cut. Of course, it takes more work to manage the two videos and extra budget if you are buying a second camera, but the end result is a very professional look.

There are a few more features I'd like you to consider adding into your video that will help give it that professional look, and it also increases engagement. Consider using animations whereby you zoom-in or pan out on an image so the video can look even more dynamic. You can also use text annotations, arrows, and circle animations to draw attention to one part of the screen or emphasize a point. I also encourage the use of lower thirds. These are graphics that appear on the lower third of your screen and can show titles/names of people on the video or even their social media handles.

Once you're adding editing and making it as refined and dynamic as you can, I want you to download it and watch the entire video all the way through to make sure there are no missed errors. If you're happy with the finished product, you're now ready to publish. Here you have several options. Most editing software can integrate and publish directly to YouTube, so that's quick and easy if you want to use that option. Alternatively, you could download it as an mp4 file and upload it directly to YouTube. Then it's time to optimize the tags, title, thumbnail, and description as we've discussed throughout this book. Keep in mind this chapter only shared extra tips and tricks that will save you time or that won't be addressed in the actual tutorial depending on the software you use. For the in-depth training of how to edit a video, I recommend watching all the get started video tutorials, follow the instructions, and give yourself time to master the process. With every video you edit and refine using these details and the new graphics and animation tips I just shared, your videos will keep getting better over time, and your brand will clearly stand out on YouTube.

10

HACKS FOR YOUTUBE CONTENT IDEAS

I t takes a lot more than consistently creating videos around your topic, editing, and publishing them to become a successful and highly paid YouTuber. The content you create needs to be amazing, and it needs to be what people are already craving to see. That implies that your best move when it comes to acquiring new subscribers comes down to finding hacks that will enable you to make engaging content.

You've come this far into the book, and you know what? You're already halfway there in relation to YouTube success because you now know the best equipment, the right mindset, the right strategy, the traffic sources to concentrate on when starting out, and even how to structure your videos properly.

What you need now is a deep dive into some more advanced ideas that can give you that extra edge. I like to see these ideas more like hacks that you can layer on once the foundation is established.

Hack #1: To create content that will get you the most attention when no one knows who you are, research, research, and research even more. That has got to become an essential aspect of your content strategy, especially in the beginning, when you're looking to get your first 1000 subscribers. Put in at least thirty minutes of research when doing your content planning, and I promise you the results will be worthwhile. Here's precisely how to go about doing this.

Let's start with the premise that YouTube acts more like Google than it does Instagram or Facebook. That means people actually search for specific keywords or phrases from their main homepage. Naturally, your video keywords will determine where it shows up on YouTube and Google search.

A neat trick here is to avoid blanket terms and high-volume short-tail keywords that have become overused. Sure it sounds like a good idea because you'll see it gets over 70k monthly searches, but you'll have a hard time ranking against millions of other videos. Instead, I want you to apply the growth formula that I shared on the section of growing your following. You want to find long-tail keywords that have high enough search volume and comparatively low search results. For example, a keyword with 1000 monthly searches and only 5000 search results on YouTube is far better for you when starting out than the 70k monthly search. Why? Your chances of ranking are higher, which means people are likely to discover your amazing content.

Keyword research tools to use:

I recommend using TubeBuddy (free on Chrome, Firefox, Android, iPhone), which is specifically made for YouTubers who want to stop wasting time optimizing their videos.

The software is accessible on your YouTube channel, where you can optimize different aspects of your video, including thumbnails. You can also check out Keywords Everywhere (free browser add on for Chrome and Firefox). This plugin used to be free but just turned into a paid software, so to get the most out of it, you will need to purchase credits. It shows you search volume and cost-per-click rates when searching on Google or YouTube. This allows you to see actual monthly search volume for any keyword or the search term as well as suggestions.

How to extract the right information.

1. Start with a broad keyword idea and type into the search box then wait for suggestions to populate.
2. For smaller channels, you can look for keywords with search volume as low as 500. You can also try using adjectives such as "best" or "easy" to see what is suggested.

On TubeBuddy, this will be easy to pull off, and you'll also find a keyword score that combines search volume and competition in the right sidebar. A good rule of thumb when starting out is to go for videos and keywords that score 30 or higher. For example, I typed in the keyword "lifestyle travel," and TubeBuddy showed me the monthly searches of that topic are 14.8K, and the score is 10. That means it is not a good idea to target because although this keyword is searched very often, it is terrible to target because it's incredibly competitive and hard to rank for.

On the other hand, the keyword "affordable luxury

travel" has 3k monthly searches with a score of 22, which isn't too bad if you're really going after a highly competitive topic like travel. Ideally, find something that has enough monthly searches and a score of 30 or what TubeBuddy considers "fair." They also provide a keyword explorer tool that helps find suggestions for video ideas and trending content based on your keyword. But remember not to opt for a video just because it's trending and has thousands of search traffic. It will do you no good to rank 25th for a high traffic keyword when you could be 5th for smaller keyword and get legit views.

When choosing your keywords, aim for the ones that you can rank for and get steady views. The more watch-time you get, the more you'll be able to rank for more competitive keywords over time.

Hack #2: Do some good YouTube video SEO so you can rank number one.

What is YouTube SEO? This is the process of optimizing your videos, playlists, and channel so you can rank higher for a chosen search query. What you need to understand is that keywords matter in your title and description. You also need to match search intent for a viewer's query, and more importantly, your video needs to be engaging enough for the search query you want to rank for. Read that last part again. Engagement is the primary intention because even if you do everything else right, but your video sucks, you won't succeed at retaining the attention of the viewer, which leads me to the next critical point.

The best way to start ranking high on YouTube organic search is to increase your watch time. It doesn't really matter how long your video is, the only thing that matters is that you can retain attention and increase watch time. That means you need to apply some of the other tactics I've already shared, such as structuring the video the right way and being thoughtful with your scripting. Once you've established this first part, the next piece is making sure you're demonstrating to both Google and YouTube that this is an engaging piece of content. An easy way to make sure people engage with you is to ask them (especially at the end of the video). Remind them to like, share, subscribe, and comment if they enjoyed watching it.

Another cool thing you can do is ask a question related to your topic so you can invite the viewers to give their input. Build your community up by encouraging participation. For example, on many of my videos, I will use graphics to ask a question like "what other tips would you add to my list?" or "what industry are you in?" I will ask my audience to comment below and encourage inter-community engagement. When I was just starting out, I searched for peers in my niche, and I made an effort to positively engage in their comments section, share my opinion and offer my input as well in a genuine and friendly way. I built rapport with the channel owners as well as the audience they were serving. Over time it helped my channel grow because we started forming YouTube pods where we started supporting each other's videos. The other piece to this tactic that is fundamental to your success is figuring out how to title your video right. The title of your video needs to incorporate the phrase or key terms that people are actually searching for. All the hard work you put in doing research and finding key words gets implemented here. The list of long-tail keywords you settled on will help form the title of your video so that when people go on Google or YouTube, they will find you. That's what video search engine optimization is all about. It doesn't need to be complicated, but you do need to apply the first hack I shared and then combine it with the suggestions mentioned here.

Hack #3: Optimize your video title and description

Once you've done research and you know the main keyphrase your audience is searching for, those words need to be included in both the title of the video as well as the first line of the video description. Your video title is the most critical piece of metadata that you can tweak and optimize to improve your results significantly. Remember, you must remain relevant by choosing a single keyphrase to optimize. The same keyword that you use on the title is also what you want to place on the description and tags sections. One more thing to remember is that once you put out the keyword (start with no more than one keyword), give it time before adjusting or adding more keywords. As you begin to drive views, you can add more keywords.

Hack #4: Optimize your thumbnail

We often hear "appearances don't count" or that we should never judge a book by its cover. Well, on YouTube, especially with new viewers, appearances do matter, and everyone judges you by your cover, i.e., your Thumbnail cover.

You need to make sure your video stands out so that

viewers can click on you instead of the thousands or sometimes millions of other search results. Thumbnails are how you make sure that click happens. It is the only thing you have control over, and it determines whether people will actually get to watch your fantastic content. Screw this one up, and it doesn't matter how great the actual video is, people will click on the video with the most appealing thumbnails.

Your thumbnail should be short, bold, and concise. It should help people know exactly what they are going to learn. More importantly, it should grab their attention from the get-go.

Because of how vital the thumbnail is to the success of your video, let's talk about the technical stuff you need to ensure you create amazing thumbnails because if you're just allowing YouTube to generate default thumbnails for you, it's going to be tough seeing fast growth on your channel.

There are two tools that I use to date, which work really well for me. Canva and Pic Monkey. If you are a pro at graphics design and don't mind having a bigger spending budget, of course, you can opt for Photoshop, but for those like me who want the simplest way to get awesome thumbnails done, just stick with one or both of these. By the way, the recommended dimension for your thumbnail is 1920 by 1080.

Hack #5: Transcribe your videos

Most YouTubers often overlook this, so if you just apply this hack alone, you will already stand out from others in your niche. Google needs as much information as possible from your video to rank it. That's why transcribing your video is so important. You can easily do this by yourself from within your creator studio by clicking on the individual video and switching on the subtitle and CC button.

Successful online marketers like Neil Patel and social media gurus like Gary Vee not only transcribe their content, but they also translate into different languages. Of course, that involves outsourcing and increasing your expenses, so you don't need to start translating into foreign languages yet until your business has grown significantly.

More Advanced Strategies to grow subscribers

Leverage psychological triggers

Scientific research proves that people are impacted and influenced by certain psychological triggers.

What that means for you is that your videos will do better when you speak to a specific group of people and trigger either their bias for influencers and celebrities or their authoritative bias trigger (just to name a few). For example, if you want to reach an audience that is hooked on the Kardashians, it might serve you well to create content where you are leveraging something that directly ties into the Kardashian.

One of my clients is a make-up artist, and she started doing tutorials on how to look exactly like Tailor Swift while spending under $10 in make-up costs. Those videos are among her best performers. That is a clear example of using influential triggers.

Another easy example where authoritative bias can be spotted is with Tai Lopez videos. When he shoots videos from his mansion or expensive cars or in a private jet, he is obviously targeting a particular group of people. His video will get over a million views, and people continue to follow him because he does a good job demonstrating that he is an authority and an expert at creating that kind of lifestyle.

Be more relatable

Now that you understand some trigger that you can start leveraging today, I want you to remember that this is about being your authentic self. Don't try to fake it till you make it. That will never work out in the long-term. You need to create content that helps people know you and your story. By creating content for a specific audience and sharing the same struggle that your audience is going through, you become very relatable, and people love to connect with those who "get them."

Video traffic hacking

Start by finding six YouTube channels similar to yours. They must be popular channels and with plenty of engagement but not necessarily big channels with millions of subscribers. The purpose of doing this is to find your peers who have created popular videos with views in the hundreds of thousands. I have found the best targets for this are channels with between 50k- 250k subscribers. For each of these six channels go to their main homepage, click on "videos" and sort by popularity. Then make an excel spreadsheet list of the top five or ten videos.

Assume that the main keyword for each video is what appears on the title because most of these YouTubers probably understand the algorithm works in your favor when you optimize the video title with the keyword. Another cool thing about using TubeBuddy is that when using it, you'll get to see which keywords the video is ranking for when you click through to start playing the video. Once you've made a list of the most viewed videos for each of the six channels, I want you to start looking out for patterns. Which keywords are prevalent across all channels? Can you spot any overlaps? We want to find the keywords that are getting massive views for everyone across the board. Then I want you to pick four or five or the winning videos and roll up your sleeves because it's time to create some epic video content.

Now that you know how to structure your video the right way and you have a script or outline, make sure you're camera-ready and that your content is better than what's already there. Find a unique angle and speak to that. Notice the gaps the other videos weren't able to fill and do your best to close those gaps for the people already searching for that topic. It's not about copying their content; it's about creating the best piece on that same topic. To make sure you do this right, let me introduce you to the concept known as the "skyscraper technique" within the blogging world. It's a term coined by Brian Dean.

He was able to build a very successful blog in a highly competitive and saturated space through this technique.

Here's how it works:

1. You need to do thorough research for your keyword on YouTube and Google. Go through the first five to ten search results and check for headlines, subheadlines, etc., especially with articles. In the case of videos, you want to take note of the points covered by the creator.
2. Check the "searched related to..." at the bottom of Google search. Also, check the "People Also Ask" suggestions on Google search.

Now you're ready to create an epic resource using the skyscraper technique. What you want to achieve is a video that goes above and beyond what's already out there. Add the unique perspective you have and fill in some of the missing gaps. You should also make yours more interactive and memorable by incorporating graphics, personal stories, and your branding style. If you can get even three of these comprehensive resources created, I guarantee you'll increase your channel watch time and video views.

Piggyback on Amazon data to create content that you know your ideal audience wants.

Another very creative way to produce content that will help you attract the attention of your ideal audience is to leverage the data Amazon has. This will take a bit of research and effort upfront, but it's well worth it, especially when you know your ideal audience well enough. Here's how to do it:

Go on Amazon find books within your niche that people are writing about and look at the 2 and 3-star reviews. The reason you want to look at the two and three stars is that people will usually rate it that bad and leave lengthy comments to share what they truly feel the book was missing. In other words, if their problem wasn't solved, you'll get to know exactly what they were hoping to get out of the book. With that knowledge, you can quickly come up with video content that addresses and resolves that problem. Then use those same keywords as the book to rank within YouTube and give people what they really want.

Promote your YouTube videos on other platforms.

Take your YouTube video and do an outreach to all the bloggers who write articles similar to the concept you taught or shared in your video. Ask the bloggers to embed that video within their article. Not everyone will agree to it, but few will. What you'll notice is your viewership will increase, which will send more positive signals to the YouTube algorithm. That tactic also helps you build backlinks, which is also great for SEO and ranking purposes.

You can also send out an email broadcast if you have an email list or share your video on Facebook, Instagram, LinkedIn or any other social platform that you may have followers and ask them to engage.

Growing your subscribers fast

Assuming you are following all the strategies this book has given you, your YouTube channel should not only be professional and highly engaging, but it should also be growing. But what happens when you've done everything right, and it's still not growing?

Recently John asked a question on the weekly mastermind that I host for my YouTube clients. He's been with us about six weeks now, and he was getting concerned about the fact that his YouTube analytics was showing that 80% of his viewers are not subscribers. His main issue now is how to get more of his audience to turn into subscribers. Part of the homework I gave him is what I am going to be sharing below, but before I do, here's something to consider. You need to always keep in mind that YouTube is a search engine. People are searching for things they need help with, so they might not even be logged into their YouTube app. Some people don't even know what they need to do to subscribe to your channel. So don't beat yourself up too much if you know you're doing everything right. The ratio of viewers to subscribers always seems off even for those of us who've been doing this for a long time.

Something else I want you to consider is the six to twelve exposure rule. In marketing, we are told that it takes at least six times of hearing a jingle on the radio before it influences your mind. In today's world, where the average American sees over five thousand ads per day, experts say it would take no less than twelve times of hearing that same jingle before it registers in the mind of the consumer. So what does this mean for you?

It means you need to be okay with the fact that people will watch your content several times before they make that commitment to become part of your YouTube tribe. Your job is to continue creating amazing content, applying everything you've learned in this book, and try to raise that exposure level.

Often I find YouTubers forgetting this one crucial thing. If you know you're doing everything right, but people aren't subscribing even if they binge-watch your videos, it's usually because you are not asking!

You must remember to regularly tell your audience the action step you want them to take. Believe it or not, people might like you and your channel, and they might watch all your videos but never subscribe because you didn't ask them to. You have to remember this whole process of watching YouTube videos is a novelty in our society. Up until 2005, this concept was non-existent. So as much as four hundred videos are being uploaded every minute, you need to remember that for the consumer, YouTube is still a new habit. This means you need to remind people to subscribe to your channel as often as possible without coming off as annoying or too pushy. Here are a few creative ways to make that "ask."

1. Tell them why they should subscribe and

what they'll get if they do. Make sure it's something worthwhile. By telling your potential subscribers exactly why they should be part of your community and the amazing benefits they get for joining your tribe, they will be more compelled to hit that subscribe button and the notifications bell.

2. Have a before, during, and after "call-to-action" asking them to subscribe but be creative with how you ask. For example, at the start of the video, you can specifically address your first-time viewers and invite them to subscribe. In the middle of the video, you can remind those that are watching that far into the video to hit that subscribe and bell if they are loving the content. You could also add a YouTube card to pop up several times with a reminder. Before you finish the video, you can create a cool graphic that also reminds the viewers to click subscribe. Be fun and creative with this.

3. Adjust your language so that you're always addressing both your existing tribe and new people who have just discovered your content for the first time. Most YouTubers forget to address and make the new viewer

feel welcome and appreciated, and that can be a turn off for someone consuming your content for the first time. Try to find that balance between using "tribe jargon" for returning followers and "welcoming" statements that encourage newbies to stick with you.

Make it easy for your audience to subscribe.

Along with making that ask in many creative ways, I also want you to make it easy for people to subscribe. Consider adding a link to every video description and let people know that it's there. You can also create playlists that you feel would be enjoyable and valuable for your audience. Invite them to watch the full playlist so they can develop that affinity and trust. In other words, find a way to sell your channel by combining the best performing videos. That might help your viewer watch more of your content and eventually lead them to subscribe because they feel the connection.

Recap of action steps for this section:

- Focus on generating traffic from search results and YouTube's suggestions sidebar.

- Find the gaps in your niche and fill them.
- Increase your watch time and session watch time as much as possible, which means spending time creating quality, engaging content.
- Prepare before getting in front of the camera with a good outline that includes the teaser, main content, a strong and clear call to action.
- Always have a hook for every video to keep viewers glued to your content. If possible, I encourage you to script your content at least until you become comfortable on camera.
- Edit your videos for that professional look and use some of the next tricks mentioned such as animations, lower thirds, and jump-cut technique to make it more engaging and dynamic.
- Don't forget to optimize your titles, tags, description, and create thumbnails that grab people's attention. Use tools like Canva for your thumbnails and take the time to create imagery that matches your brand style so people can get used to identify with your brand.
- Research, research, and do more research to

ensure you are creating searchable content, popular content, and videos that viewers actually want to watch. That will increase the likelihood of ranking faster and growing your channel quickly.

SECTION FOUR: MONETIZE YOUR YOUTUBE CHANNEL

11

HOW TO MONETIZE YOUR YOUTUBE CHANNEL

In this section, we focus on making you money. I know you care about creating an epic channel and becoming a YouTube superstar because you're on a mission to touch lives, but let's be real, making money on your channel is how you'll be able to keep going and fulfill that mission. Monetization is a vast topic. When you can successfully do it, you'll be able to turn your passion and earn a living doing what you love instead of trying to juggle a job and your YouTube activities.

I must warn you though; making money on YouTube is not as easy as marketing gurus have led you to believe. Impact and income don't just fall on your lap. Historically, most YouTubers struggle to monetize their content and efforts through the regular routes that are usually recommended. That's why I want to focus on more than just the standard YouTube monetization route that many talk about. I want to share with you how I am making money without the commonly encouraged YouTube monetization strategy that usually involves Google AdSense. Before we get to my recommended strategies, let's start with the YouTube Partner Program that everyone talks about.

What YouTube wants you to know about making money through their partner program:

Before you can start making money through YouTube's partner program, you need an audience, you need to make videos consistently that viewers really like watching and like anything else on the platform, make sure you're following the YouTube community guidelines.

Once you build momentum and tick all those boxes, you need to apply to join YouTube's partner program (YPP), which lets creators monetize their videos on YouTube. There's a certain threshold you must meet that YouTube has set in place to ensure they have enough information to review your channel and figure out if you are a good citizen in their platform. Let's talk about their main requirements.

YouTube Partner Program Requirements

Commonly known as YPP by YouTubers, there are four things you need to do before you can be eligible to start monetizing your videos.

First, you need to be in good standing with YouTube.

Second, you need to hit the milestone of 1000 subscribers. It doesn't matter how long it takes you to hit that number. What matters is that you get there. Once you do, it's time to apply and get your pass from the YouTube team.

Third, you will need 4000 hours of public watch time, which we discussed in an earlier chapter. The 4,000 hours must be within 12 months. Many people get confused about this, so let's clarify a few things. It's not about how many videos you watched or how many videos you've published (although it does help to have more content). Instead, it is about how many hours of your video, people from all over the world have consumed on your channel in the last twelve months. Again, here's something I don't want you to get confused about - even if you have more than four thousand hours since launching your channel, the only hours that matter when it comes to getting your YPP are the accumulated hours over the last twelve months. So you need to make sure you intentionally accumulate those four thousand hours within twelve months before applying for this. Live stream and unlisted videos do help add to that total watch time; just make sure not to delete any of them because once you delete any video, the watch time also disappears.

How does the money roll in with YouTube ads?

The average CPM (Cost Per Mille), which by the way can be different depending on your country and niches is that you get $2 per 1000 CPM. So, for example, if your goal is to earn $1000 per month, you would need to get 500,000 CPM.

I think a lot of people shy away from understanding the real game behind earning a good income on YouTube because they don't take the time to get real and have a very candid conversation about the dream they are going after. So let me help you out by doing an illustrative math example to ensure you understand what you're signing up for when you choose to make your main strategy AdSense and YPP. The average view is approximately 3 minutes.

This means to qualify for those 4,000 hours, you would need 240,000 minutes or 80,000 total views. The income you would get out of reaching that level and getting that 4,000hours from AdSense is, on average, $160. This is where this strategy breaks for me because, in my reasoning, it makes more sense to focus on building a successful YouTube channel for influence rather than AdSense income. You could easily get a job and make even more than what AdSense gives you. I feel it would be such a slow, hard grind to depend entirely on your YouTube marketing if this is the only monetization strategy you deploy. If you agree with me that the YouTube AdSense strategy is the least favorable way to earn a full-time income, then let me share with you other ways you can focus on to make crazy money.

Insider hack:

Just because I don't believe in YPP doesn't mean you can't go after it. And if you do, I encourage you to learn from a fellow YouTuber's strategy and niche down your channel to focus on the topics that have higher CPMs because not all CPMs pay $2. Some pay as high as $15 CPM. The key strategy is to focus on getting the highest number of views because that directly impacts your income. For example, James has a niched e-commerce channel, and he is earning decent money each month using YouTube Ads. James usually gets about 160,000 views in a month, which leads to estimated revenue of a little over $1,000 mainly because he is super niched on a topic that pays him $15 CPM. So if you can really niche your channel down and go into specific niches that already have a high CPM, then you can start earning some good money. But remember, these examples are just for illustration purposes, not a promise to you. If you want to be as successful as James, you will need to put in a lot of hard work and take massive action.

CREATIVE WAYS TO MAKE MONEY ON YOUTUBE

Affiliate Marketing

I believe this is literally the best way to get started, especially if you don't have a product or service created yet. I recommend starting with Amazon Affiliates because it is probably one of the best affiliate programs you can quickly jump on today. With over three hundred million active users on this platform, chances are, your viewers already have an Amazon account. More importantly, it is the most convenient and globally trusted way to shop easily online, so there's very little friction for your audience as long as you do things right. All you need to do is create your Amazon affiliate account, link different items from Amazon into your YouTube videos, and create epic content that resonates with the products you're selling. Then, viewers can click directly to the page using your affiliate link to make a purchase, and just like that, you make money.

For example, in our YouTube mastermind, we have a member who is passionate about Barbeques. So he started a BBQ channel last year. Each week he shoots a video either talking about a new BBQ accessory that he's using or giving a step-by-step BBQ cooking lesson. One of his best performing videos is reviewing a BBQ grill accessory that he gifted his dad on Father's Day. On the description link, the first line has his Amazon affiliate link, and he's making about $500 each month on that single BBQ grill accessory alone. Here's the cool part that even he didn't see coming. Now that he's been doing this for over a year and because he's so niched down, he has started getting free stuff being offered to him by people who are within that same niche. He recently got a meat sponsor, i.e., a meat supplier sends him free meat for his cooking tutorials. He also got a new grill last month, which was given as a gift by a new supplier.

Insider hack:

There's an affiliate program for almost any niche you can think of. Some will make you more money than others, and the more research you do to find the best affiliate deals, the more money you could potentially earn. Google the brand you love or want to create content around and type in affiliate, or ambassador or associate program.

The best types of videos for affiliate marketing include product reviews or product tutorials. These are a few examples of affiliate video content you can create. I hope you're starting to see some of the good that can come your way if you nail down your niche, align it with some affiliate marketing, and produce content that engages your audience.

Sell Your Own Product or Service

If you're going through the trouble of building a channel, you should have a strategy for selling something. I want you to step away from thinking small, i.e., YouTube Ads and AdSense money to thinking big. Thinking big means that from day one, you will be playing on the platform with the intention of selling something you have full ownership of. Even if you don't quite know what you will create and sell yet. If you're going to become a YouTube superstar and build a business around your channel or brand, you have to develop a business model. Unless you have a business plan, this will never really become a real business that gives you the freedom and lifestyle you desire. Selling your own product or service is something I highly recommend you do as part of your business model.

For example, another member of our YouTube mastermind Time created his own line of merchandise by going to teespring.com and uploaded some artwork design. Now he has a whole collection that people can buy with just a single click online. Susan, who is an artist, does something similar, but she set up shop on Etsy and drives people to her online store where they can purchase her artworks. So when you're thinking about creating a product or service, don't over complicate things. Study your audience, figure out what they would love to have, do lots of tests and experiments before investing in something huge, and then make a product. If you want to monetize your expertise, consider packaging a service, like a done for your service or consultation service. You could even build an evergreen online course and make that your signature product.

How Eileen is making an income as a fulltime YouTuber

Eileen has a small channel that gets hundreds of views for each video, and she's a fulltime YouTuber. She's niched down within the personal development and wellness space, which has allowed her to generate income consistently. How? Because she's created a book that's currently selling on Amazon for $6 and she's got an evergreen online course that dives deeper into the same topic, which goes for $197. Then she produces high-value content and coaching videos that help touch on the same pain points that both her book and online course cover. When she started, she had no idea how to write a book or build an online course. But she stuck with it and figured it out. So can you.

How I made over $30,000 in one year

Once you gain traction on YouTube, you will essentially experience what I call the snowball effect, just as I did. Think of how that metaphor works. At first, when you are pushing and trying to gain momentum, it's hard because it's like rolling a snowball up the top of a mountain. But if you can persevere and keep going eventually, you'll get to the point where the snowball takes off rolling down on its own momentum, and gravity seems to help it grow and get faster exponentially. That is what I think it's like to become successful on YouTube. At first, it was a rough mountain climb with a lot of resistance. Then once I hit my stride, I ended up making over $30k in just twelve months without needing to work hard. Today, YouTube activities are responsible for over 50% of all my online income. Not because my six published books or my online courses have stopped making money but because YouTube has grown and continues to grow so fast because I finally got traction.

Make no mistake; you can make a lot of money on YouTube. But before that can happen, you really must understand the business model you're building and your potential income sources. If you're going to wait around for YouTube ads to make you rich, you'll be waiting a really long time. That's why my best advice is to build multiple income streams. It will not only make you as much money as possible, but as well, it will mitigate your risk because you'll be diversifying your income. All wealthy people have multiple streams of income. It's the great secret held by the top income earners of this world. Do you know how Jay-Z became a billionaire in 2019? By having multiple income streams.

Think of social media gurus like Tai Lopez, Gary Vee, or Seth Godin, and it will all start to make sense when you peel back their business model. Although they like to exaggerate on specific topics or sell you the latest and greatest shiny system or marketing strategy, the truth of the matter is, they are successful because of all the "behind the scenes" work they do that is often totally non-related to the topics that go viral on social media. In other words, even if they do invest in a particular activity or channel, it's only one of many other income-producing activities that they are involved in. So before you spend the next three years trying hard to make YPP make you enough money to quit your job or travel more, let's look at the income sources I have leveraged to give me a steady paycheck. I will share with you the pros and cons so you can make an informed decision on the best options to leverage in your business.

- YouTube Ads
- Sponsorships
- Affiliates
- Super Chat

- Own Product or Service
- Patreon

YouTube ads

We already talked about how you can make money using YPP, which is essentially AdSense. Whenever you see a video titled "How I make money on YouTube," it's almost always entirely about YouTube ads. So a lot of creators think that ads are the only way to make money. As you learned earlier, you need to reach a certain threshold before that's even possible, and the income you get is pretty low, which is why many creators aren't making that much money. They are dependent on this one monetization tactic. While I am not discouraging you from adding this to your monetization strategy, I urge you to think bigger. I still have YouTube ads running in my business strategy. In fact, I was able to start monetizing my channel almost ten months from starting it. Monthly video views were around 170,000, so the channel was snowballing, but that still only translated to under $2,000 per month. For the lifestyle I wanted to have, it wouldn't be plausible to be a fulltime YouTuber. That's why I had to find other alternatives. My best options to date are affiliate sales and sponsorships. This leads me to my next point.

Sponsorships

Movie stars, athletes, and television stars do it all the time. The good news is, anyone with enough influence and a handful of followers on social media can now do it too. Social media influencers are now receiving the same celebrity-like status as traditional celebrities, which is so cool. As a YouTube creator, sponsorships from companies will become one of your biggest income sources if you play your cards right.

There are three types of sponsorships that I am aware of. You can either get paid an agreed-upon fee to produce a video or series of videos. You can also get free products, or you can receive a base fee plus commission on clicks or sales for a video or series. Free products are okay. They can be a significant compensation, especially if you're just starting out, and I encourage you to leverage that until you have enough credibility and influence to demand a direct fee. To get free products do a little homework on channels that are reviewing products or services within your niche. Make a list of the companies, go to their website, and do some data mining for their contact details. Send them a well-crafted email detailing your interest and why they should consider using your channel. Make sure you focus on what's in it for them if they agree to do business with you.

Given that I know how validating it is to get paid to shoot a video, my focus here will be on paid sponsorships. Efforts that will directly result in a happy bank statement at the end of the month. What you need to do is follow the same approach and tactics as the free products strategy and just knock on as many relevant doors as you can. You can also plan to attend conferences within your local area and do some in-person networking. With a little creativity, you can even demonstrate to them why they should be working with you by shooting an epic trailer and sharing it with them. It helps if you can back up your proposal with real data to validate the value of your channel.

There are two types of videos you can create for a sponsor. A general interest video related to the sponsor or a direct review video. The general interest video is usually broad and appeals to a broader audience. It also doesn't come across as too commercialized or overly salesly. However, it still allows you to mention the company a couple of times, and if you carefully craft the content and make it valuable, your audience will appreciate the content and engage more with the sponsor's pitch. This is where the power of storytelling comes in. Choose to work with brands that allow you to collaborate on something that is authentic and aligns with your personality and how you naturally communicate with your audience. Otherwise, you stand the chance of losing the respect and influence of your tribe. Let's suppose your channel is for baking enthusiasts. You might do a video with Halloween cupcakes that have certain fillings in them, and you can recommend the specific brand that you've partnered with. You mention the brand a couple of times, naturally talking about them as your recommended option and the benefits of using that brand instead of others.

This is an excellent example of how to execute this general interest strategy. As you can see, it adds lots of value to your audience because you show them how to make epic cupcakes, and you also promote your sponsor without commercializing it.

To execute on the direct review strategy, you would need to directly talk about the brand itself, the benefits, and maybe even showcase the various products they have and how a viewer can use them to make various types of cupcakes and cakes. You can walk your audience through the "unboxing" dissect the various ingredients used in the pack etc. The benefit of a direct review is that you're more likely to rank for that keyword and have a higher CTR and conversion, especially if you do great job story-telling. When you can show sponsors how easily you can get them results through these two videos (I recommend combining both), generating consistent income will be a natural by-product.

I know what you're thinking, how do I get hard data for my pitch when I haven't signed a deal with any company. Easy. Through your Affiliate marketing strategy. Any affiliate sales you make can be tracked using tools like PrettyLink. Once you have this data and you know your click-through rate (CTR), you can use this data to make your pitch and prove that your stuff converts. Sponsors love to see conversion data.

Affiliate sales

This is my best strategy, which is why I also went into great detail on how you can do it in a previous chapter. Affiliate marketing is the easiest way for you to start monetizing your channel regardless of subscriber size and watch time. Of course, the more engagement and influence you have, the better your chances of selling more. You can find all kinds of products around your niche, and sometimes it doesn't even need to be directly within your niche, it could be something related to your niche that you know your audience needs. For example, think back to the example I gave you of the YouTuber with a BBQ channel. He gets sponsored by a meat supplier and affiliates for BBQ accessories as well as cleaning products. I know, sounds crazy, right? But think about it for a minute. If you are going to BBQ and you're passionate about doing it right, you probably also care about proper cleaning and maintenance of your equipment. He found a great deal from a small organic local cleaning supplier and now incorporates that "related" product into some of his videos. The commissions on that are incredible because it's a direct deal with a local shop. That's just one example. Think of how many related products or services you can create affiliate agreements that all help your client solve a specific problem they are already having, and you can cash-in faster than you initially imagined. When it comes to affiliate marketing, your imagination is the only limit.

How to determine what to charge for your sponsorship deals

This is a question I get asked a lot, and to be honest, there is no hard answer. What you charge depends on a lot of things. How much experience you have, your niche, the success you've had with your past campaigns, the effort needed to make it work, etc. A smart way to estimate a fair price is to look at the data of your click-through-rates and conversions for your videos through affiliates you've done. Otherwise, a good rule of thumb is a CTR of between 5% - 10%. I've also seen YouTubers charge an average of between $0.05 to $0.15 per view. So it all depends on how you feel comfortable structuring this. Also, if you can be able to combine sponsorship and affiliate commissions within the same deal, I recommend going for that. The upfront fee for sponsorship might be lower, and that's okay. What you get in the back end if you do your job right will be far more money than that single sponsored fee.

Always disclose paid agreements.

By law and YouTube, you are required to disclose that you have received compensation whenever you make these types of videos. You should do this verbally in the video as well as through YouTube's sponsor declaration in the video's "Advanced Settings."

Super Chat

This is a fresh new way to make additional money that I recently started doing as well. It is a viewer sponsorship that happens during Live streaming. In essence, it's donating to the creator. The viewer "buys" a Super Chat, and they get a chance to interact with you directly as well as support the channel and your work through that donation which can be as little as $5.

The downside, if you will, is that YouTube takes 30% of your Super Chat revenue and passes the remaining on to you through your AdSense account. One of the benefits of Super Chatting as a viewer is that you not only support your favorite channel, but you also get a "spotlight," and your comments get highlighted in a different color, which immediately makes you stand out and often leads to a direct shout-out from the creator. This is only available through the live stream, so if you're not regularly doing this and already have an engaged audience, it probably won't be much of an income source. I do encourage you to build up to it.

Patreon

This is another popular income stream many YouTubers are leveraging today. The website is based on the old system of patronage that many artists and other types of artists have been using for decades. If you want to see a channel that does it really well I suggest you check out HAS Fit because their entire channel is based on this system. How it works is someone chooses to support you with a monthly income in exchange for rights or just to enjoy the videos you create. In the renaissance era, where it was most famous, artists like Michelangelo and Botticelli used it. Today, YouTube has made it possible for creators to enjoy the same benefits, and it can actually generate a substantial income if you have a good strategy. If you are interested in this, all you would need to do is create a page on Patreon and offer extras to patrons in tiers. These can be exclusive videos that can't be publically accessed or early access or group meetings.

The downside to using this is that it doesn't seem to be much money compared to other income sources, and the platform also charges a fee, although it is much less than what you pay for a Super Chat. I think what makes this worthwhile or not is your ability to convert a lot of people over to your Patreon page.

Selling your own products.

This strategy makes a lot of sense because you can really cash in quick and with very high margins. It also works really well because people on your channel are more likely to trust you or at least have some brand affinity. That's how you can quickly earn some serious cash with a small subscriber base and a low reach. I already talked about this before, so instead, let me give you more ideas on what you can sell as well as some downfalls to become aware of. You can sell merchandise like t-shirts, artworks, and mugs with your design or logo printed. You could also sell books, paid video courses, or services like one-to-one consulting if you're a professional in a particular field. I've seen a lot of smaller channels grow their income exponentially with masterminds and weekly group meetings. There's no end to what you can sell.

The downside the effort, time, and resources it takes to create a marketing funnel that works and in some cases, a product or service that works. If you consider the time it would take to develop, package and market something you create from scratch versus other income sources such as affiliates or sponsorships, it's a no brainer. The learning curve is more significant, and so is the risk. So when you're just starting out, I encourage you to be strategic. Think big and then take small actions until you finally have the kind of business that will give you the lifestyle you've been dreaming of.

Recap of action steps for this section:

1. There are various ways to monetize your YouTube channel. The most common one is by applying for YPP. However, you must meet all the requirements before you can qualify. The amount of money you make will depend on the CMP of your niche, so try to go for niches that pay-out higher CPMs.

2. The best way to monetize your channel, in my opinion, is through combining affiliates and sponsorships deals. It's fast, easy to set up and execute, and you don't need a huge tribe or lots of traffic to succeed.

3. If you have the time, knowledge, skillset, and patience, consider developing and selling your own product or service. The profit margins are higher, and you will have full ownership.

4. Research no less than six similar channels that are already monetizing either through affiliates or sponsorship to gather data on the best companies to start doing an outreach campaign. Once you have the list, craft an effective outreach campaign and pitch yourself and your channel with hard data.

AFTERWORD

It has taken me hundreds of videos and thousands of hours of making content on YouTube to figure out some of the secrets I've shared with you on this book. There's one last secret I want to share with you before you go out there and crush it. It has become so obvious and so clear to me recently, what is genuinely catapulting people on this platform and enabling them to go from zero subscribers and income to tens of thousands in both revenue and loyal fans.

The base knowledge of what works on this platform will always be the same. There are many variables that you won't be able to control as you grow your channel. You can't control the algorithm or who sees you or how many viewers you get. The only thing you can control (and the final secret I will be sharing with you), which is also the greatest asset you have is - You.

You are the determining factor in your ability to succeed in this competitive space. The thing that's holding people back from succeeding on YouTube is their inability to maximize who they are. I must confess, it has taken me a long time to figure it out. This has been my lesson too. As my channel grew, I have tried every different kind of iteration there is (sometimes copying other famous YouTubers), and here's what I've learned - You need to shift focus from external growth and focus on internal growth. I have stopped trying to compare myself, my set, my equipment, my style of teaching, etc. with other YouTubers and have started being really authentic and focusing solely on my internal growth.

Don't make the same mistake. On YouTube, you win by being yourself and paying attention to what works for you and what your audience wants. We all tend to try so hard to be something that we're not, and it makes the whole process harder than it needs to be. Find what works best for you, be true to yourself, and play to your strengths. YouTube is about being originally YOU. The things that make you unique, the things that make you different and quirky are the reason you're going to be successful. It may not feel like that right now, but if you pay attention to the top 1% of YouTube superstars, it will become evident to you. If there's one thing I can't stress enough, it is this: The growth you are looking for is right in front of you.

You can be from any walk of life, any background, any gender, any ethnicity, and you have the opportunity of a lifetime. This is the best time for you to succeed, and you have everything you need to win really big and gain a lot of influence while making a lot of money on this platform.

When it comes to growing and scaling your YouTube channel, remember this. It is going to take time, effort, and the right strategy. There's no magic bullet. It's important to pace yourself when starting out so that you don't make the mistake of over-stretching yourself and setting false expectations. Sure it would be great to hear that you went from zero to 100,000 subscribers in ten months, but I wouldn't recommend setting that as your goal.

Treat it like a real business:

When someone starts a traditional brick and mortar

business, the expectations within the first twelve months are always underrated because everyone knows it takes time and effort to make a business succeed. You need to treat your online business the same way. YouTube will work for you, but only if you set it up for success. If you expect to reap what you have not sowed just because gurus call it a gold mine, you will be disappointed. Everything I have shared in this book is to help you sow and reap a plentiful harvest in monetary form and a loyal fanbase. The platform will continue to change, and the tactics will adjust accordingly. Still, the strategy of winning and succeeding will always remain the same. As long as you keep your head in the game, focus on serving and growing your audience, and delivering the best content possible to that chosen audience, you will always have a thriving channel. You now have all the strategies needed to build a successful channel that makes you money, it's your turn to roll up those sleeves and become a YouTuber moneymaker.

RESOURCES

James, S. (2019, November 8). 5 YouTube Tips For Beginners. Retrieved November 21, 2019, from https://projectlifemastery.com/5-youtube-tips-for-beginners/

YouTube Creator Academy Quickstart Guide. (n.d.). Retrieved November 21, 2019, from https://creatoracademy.youtube.com/page/course/bootcamp-foundations

YouTube. (n.d.). Retrieved November 21, 2019, from https://www.youtube.com/watch?v=aB0TlsnkY6E

Think Media. (2019). How To Make A YouTube Video (Beginners Tutorial) [YouTube]. Retrieved November 21, 2019, from https://www.youtube.com/watch?v=aB0TlsnkY6E&feature=youtu.be

Hogue, J. H. (2019). *Crushing YouTube.* Retrieved from My Book

Cannell Travis, S. C. B. T. (2018). *YouTube Secrets.* Retrieved from My Book

CPSIA information can be obtained
at www.ICGtesting.com
Printed in the USA
LVHW032330180820
663389LV00003B/178

9 781989 638651